h.D.

American History 1877 to the Present

Second Edition

BARRON'S

All inquiries should be addressed to:
Barron's Educational Series, Inc.
250 Wireless Boulevard
Hauppauge, New York 11788
http://www.barronseduc.com

Library of Congress Catalog Card No. 2002035384

ISBN-13: 978-0-7641-2005-3
ISBN-10: 0-7641-2005-0

Library of Congress Cataloging-in-Publication Data
Capozzoli Ingui, Mary Jane.
    American history, 1877 to the present / Mary Jane Capozzoli Ingui.—2nd ed.
        p. cm.—(Barron's EZ 101 study keys)
    Includes index.
    ISBN 0-7641-2005-0 (alk. paper)
        1. United States—History—1865—Study and teaching. 2. United States—
    History—1865—Outlines, syllabi, etc. I. Title. II. Series.

    E661. C27   2003
    973.8'071'1—dc21   2002035384

CONTENTS

Theme 1 THE NEW SOUTH AND WESTERN DEVELOPMENT

*T*he years after Reconstruction were characterized by the expansion and development of America's emerging urban-industrial society. They were also marked by an agricultural revolution, which involved the invention and application of machinery to agriculture, along with the development of scientific agriculture.

During the second half of the nineteenth century, the South attempted to transform itself into a modern, industrial region while also rebuilding its agrarian economy. Yet, at the century's end, the New South retained its second-class status because it continued to lag behind the North in both agricultural and industrial development.

At the same time, in the New West, the area beyond the Mississippi River, whites (native born and immigrants) as well as some blacks poured into the region, struggling against natural obstacles and clashing with native Americans of the region. By 1900, this new region consisted of farms, ranches, mining operations, and cities, all with a distinctive American character.

INDIVIDUAL KEYS IN THIS THEME

1	Change in the South
2	Treatment of blacks and response
3	Transformation of the West
4	Native Americans of the West
5	Indian response to white incursion

Key 1   Change in the South

OVERVIEW *Many important political, economic, and social changes took place in the New South after Reconstruction.*

Politics: For Southern whites, the Democratic Party emerged as the only viable political organization.
- To ensure its control, each Southern state passed legislation which took voting rights away from blacks.
- Examples included the literacy test, the poll tax, and the "grandfather clause."

Economics: Economic systems that gave whites ownership of most of the land, while blacks became tenants and sharecroppers, were perpetuated.

Social: The white leadership adopted Jim Crow laws that required racial separation of public facilities. Most political and economic power remained with the powerful white aristocracy.

"Redeemers" and "Bourbons": Terms used to describe the powerful, conservative oligarchy that controlled every Southern state government during the post-Reconstruction period.
- Although at times this ruling class was similar to the antebellum planter class, it often consisted of merchants, industrialists, railroad developers, or financiers.
- Some had been planters, but others were often immigrants from the North or upwardly mobile white Southerners.
- Bourbon governments were usually corrupt and curtailed state services, lowered taxation, and reduced spending.

Joel Chandler Harris and Uncle Remus (1880): A writer whose tales, such as *Uncle Remus,* depicted the antebellum slave society as a harmonious world. Such nostalgic portraits of the Old South in literature were very popular and were an indication of the role and the power of the Southern past.

Mill towns: The most visible signs of Southern industrial expansion after Reconstruction.
- Textile factories were encouraged by Southern conservative governments, which could offer low taxes, a cheap labor supply, and an abundance of water power.

- The tobacco processing industry, the iron industry, and the development of railroads were other examples of Southern industrial growth.
- Mill towns controlled their workers' lives. While providing community and solidarity among workers, mill towns prevented union organization.
- Company stores charged inflated prices for their goods and issued exorbitant rates of credit to workers.
- These one-industry towns did not allow competitors to establish plants.

Crop-lien system: Central to Southern agriculture, a method by which a farmer mortgaged his ungrown crop to obtain use of the land and necessary supplies from the owner of a local store selling tools or seed.
- Since these merchants seldom had competitors, farmers had little choice but to pay inflated prices for goods purchased on credit.
- They also paid high interest so that, when they harvested their crops, they were often so deeply in debt that giving the entire harvest to the merchant was not enough to settle the account.
- Each year their indebtedness grew, and farmers often lost their land; farmers who were already tenants held little hope of ever paying off their debts.
- This system of economic tyranny contributed to an increase in the cultivation of cash crops because they were viewed as a more lucrative means of paying one's debts.

Key 2   Treatment of blacks and

response

OVERVIEW *Southern states passed laws that discriminated against blacks, and the U.S. government supported segregation by its court decisions.*

Jim Crow laws: Passed by one Southern state after another, beginning in 1881.
- These laws instituted racial segregation of public facilities.
- By the 1890s, the Supreme Court had validated such legislation (see below).
- Reaching into almost every area of Southern life, these laws provided a means for whites to retain control of social relations between the races in the urban and rural south.

Plessy **v.** *Ferguson* **(1896):** This landmark Supreme Court case involved a law that required separate seating for blacks and whites on railroads.
- The Court decided that separate accommodations did not deprive blacks of equal rights if the accommodations were equal.
- The decision survived as the legal basis for segregated schools until the landmark decision of *Brown* **v.** *Board of Education* in 1954.

Williams **v.** *Mississippi* **(1898):** This case validated literacy tests for voting and thus illustrated the Court's willingness to let Southern states define their own suffrage standards, even at the expense of blacks.

Cumming **v.** *Board of Education* **(1899):** This case laid the foundation for segregated schools. The Court held that laws establishing separate schools for whites were valid even if they provided no comparable schools for blacks.

Lynchings: White violence against blacks increased as another means of controlling blacks through terror and intimidation and inhibiting their agitation for equal rights.
- The prime example of such violence involved lynching of blacks by white vigilante mobs.
- Black prisoners or blacks simply accused of crimes were sometimes executed in public rituals.

- During the 1890s there were about 187 lynchings each year, over four-fifths in the South.

Ida B. Wells-Barnett: A black journalist who launched an international antilynching movement whose goal was a federal antilynching law.

Booker T. Washington: A chief spokesman for the black middle class that emerged in the New South.
- He was the founder and president of Tuskegee Institute in Alabama.
- His self-improvement message urged blacks to seek a technical, rather than a classical, education.
- He believed that by adopting white middle-class standards in speech, dress, and habits, blacks would gain the respect of whites.
- In his philosophy of race relations, known as the **Atlanta Compromise,** he advocated the pursuit of economic gains for blacks as a step toward the attainment of social equality.

W. E. B. DuBois: A leading black critic of Booker T. Washington.
- He urged the **"talented tenth"** of the black race to attend college and become professionals.
- These blacks should lead the fight for the immediate restoration of their civil rights.
- In 1905 DuBois founded the **Niagara movement,** which argued against the accommodationist tactics of Washington.
- The group's "Declaration of Principles" demanded suffrage and civil rights by opposing Jim Crown laws.

NAACP (1909): W. E. B. DuBois's Niagara movement provided the groundwork for the creation of the **National Association for the Advancement of Colored People (NAACP).**
- This was an interracial organization whose goal was the attainment of equal rights for blacks through the use of lawsuits in federal courts.
- It opposed the political and economic subordination of blacks for promoting the leadership of a trained, black elite.

KEY QUOTATION

The Fourteenth Amendment was intended to enforce the absolute equality of the two races . . . but not to abolish distinctions based upon color. . . .

> Court establishment of "separate but equal" doctrine
> *Plessy* v. *Ferguson,* 1896

Key 3 Transformation of the West

OVERVIEW *Although the Great Plains and the Great Basin were the home of nomadic native American tribes and wild animals, by the 1890s the great migration of pioneers had established a line of settlement to the Pacific coast. Migrants to the West were attracted by gold and silver deposits, railroad lines, and the federal government's land policy.*

Homestead Act (1862): Allowed settlers to buy 160 acres for a small fee if they occupied and improved it for 5 years.
- The act served as an impetus to Western settlement, and some 400,000 **homesteaders** became landowners.
- The bleak life on the Great Plains, however, caused most homesteaders to abandon their property.

Morrill Land Grant Act (1862): Provided that federal land be used to finance land grant **agricultural colleges**. Scientific and mechanical methods of farming were taught and were responsible for the development of the agricultural Midwest.

Timber Culture Act (1873): Passed as an amendment to the Homestead Act, it allowed homesteaders to receive grants of an additional 160 acres if they planted 40 acres of trees on the land within 4 years.

Desert Land Act (1877): Resulted in the purchase of 2.5 million acres of Western land.
- Anyone could secure tentative title to 640 acres in the Great Plains or Southwest for 25 cents an acre.
- After irrigating a portion of the land within 3 years, the settler could receive full title to the land for another $1.00 per acre.

Timber and Stone Act (1878): Authorized sales of barren land at $2.50 an acre.

Mining towns: As in the California gold rush of 1849 and the Colorado rush of 1859, the mineral-rich areas of the West were the first to be extensively settled.
- Following prospectors and commercial miners came ranchers and farmers.
- Copper, lead, tin, quartz, and zinc proved to be more profitable than gold and silver in the long term.

- These communities were melting pots containing native Americans, Mexicans, blacks, Chinese, and white; there were few women.

Cattle industry: A significant element in the West's economy.
- Mexican ranchers had developed the ranching techniques that were subsequently utilized first by Texans, then by Great Plains cattlemen and cowboys.
- During the 1860s, the **long drive** came into being as cattle were driven to distant markets and pastured along the trial.
- By the 1970s special market facilities for cattle were established at Abilene, Kansas, on the Kansas Pacific Railroad.
- Other trails and market outlets were created (e.g., Dodge City, Kansas; Cheyenne, Wyoming) to rival Abilene.
- Two severe winters (1885–86 and 1886–87) and a scorching summer marked the decline of the open-range cattle industry and the end of the long drive.

Cowboys: Integral to the long drive, cowboys were often veterans of the Confederate Army, white Northerners, Mexicans, or foreigners, with freed blacks comprising the next largest group.

Owen Wister: Author of a western novel, *The Virginian,* which typified the romance of the West by painting an idealized picture of the rugged, free-spirited cowboy. Representing the ideal of the "natural man," the cowboy became a revered American symbol.

Mark Twain: One of the greatest American writers of the nineteenth century and the author of a series of novels (e.g., *The Adventures of Tom Sawyer, Huckleberry Finn*) during the 1870s and 1880s that depicted the vision and spirit of the frontier West.

Frederick Jackson Turner: Historian from the University of Wisconsin whose paper, **"The Significance of the Frontier,"** argued that the closing of the frontier had ended an era in American history.
- Using the census report of 1890, Turner explained that the settlement of the frontier had provided an explanatory framework for American development.
- His work also illustrates the psychological power of the frontier in that, with its passing, Americans began to realize that revitalizing opportunities were also vanishing.

Key 4 Native Americans of the West

OVERVIEW *Lands west of the Mississippi were home to Western tribes such as the **Pueblo, Navajo, Apache,** and **Sioux,** as well as Eastern tribes—**Cherokee, Creek, Winnebago**—that had been forcibly resettled in the West.*

Life-styles: Reflecting various life-styles, some native Americans were farmers and had permanent settlements, while others lived nomadically, combining hunting with farming and sheep herding.

The Plains Indian culture: Plains Indians constituted the largest group in the West. Often militant warriors, they were in the vanguard of the struggle to defend their lands from white settlement.
- Their nomadic life in harmony with nature depended upon the **buffalo,** or **bison,** because, as a source of food, clothing, fuel, and weapons, it provided the economic basis for their lives.
  - Their society was organized into tribes, which were usually subdivided into "bands" of about 500 men and women, each with a governing council.
  - Women assumed domestic and artistic roles, while men hunted, traded, and supervised religious and military life.
  - Each tribe's warrior class competed with others to establish a reputation for bravery.
  - These Western tribes never successfully united politically or militarily against white power, thus contributing to their defeat by the white society.

Government policy toward the native American: The federal government traditionally regarded Indian tribes both as **independent nations** and as **wards** and therefore negotiated treaties with them that required ratification by the Senate.
- Western tribes were often victimized by incompetent white officials charged with protecting them.
- As white settlers moved west, they exerted more and more pressure for access to Indian lands.
- The government frequently responded by violating treaties they had made with Native Americans.

Concentration policy: This policy, associated with the 1850s, resulted in a **reservation policy**.
- The creation of Indian reservations allowed the government to force tribes into scattered locations, often with land unfitted for agriculture.
- The most desirable lands were retained for white settlement.

Relocation: In 1867, an **Indian Peace Commission,** established by Congress, decided that all Plains tribes would be relocated on two reservations, one in **Oklahoma** and the other in the **Dakotas.**
- **The Bureau of Indian Affairs** in the Department of the Interior was in charge of the reservations.
- Poor administration by this agency resulted in constant conflicts between tribes and nearby white settlers.

Tribal independence ceased to be recognized: The federal government also decided that it would no longer recognize tribes as independent entities or negotiate with tribal chiefs. This signaled the beginning of efforts aimed at undermining the **collective nature** of Indian life, thereby forcing **assimilation** into the white culture.

The buffalo: The welfare of native Americans was also greatly affected by the mass slaughter of buffalo from the 1850s onward.
- Migrants and professional hunters virtually exterminated whole herds, which were obstacles to railroad traffic.
- **Buffalo Bill Cody,** for instance, was hired by railroad companies to kill buffalo.
- The U.S. Army and agents of the Bureau of Indian Affairs also encouraged the slaughter.
- The killing of buffalo resulted in many Indian uprisings in an effort to preserve their way of life.

Key 5   Indian response to white incursion

OVERVIEW *Native Americans were unable to resist the superior numbers and technology of the white society and were forced to accept settlement on whatever lands the U.S. government was willing to give them. Formal warfare between Indians and whites ended by 1886, when* **Geronimo,** *an* **Apache** *chief in the Southwest, surrendered to white forces.*

Indian resistance to white settlement: Indian response emerged from the 1850s to the 1880s and focused on wagon trains, stagecoaches, white soldiers, and scattered settlements.
* By the 1860s the U.S. Army conducted most of the warfare against Western Indians.
* Fighting was usually small scale.
* The last native Americans to maintain organized resistance against whites were the Apaches, who fought into the 1880s.

Battle of Little Bighorn (1876): One of the most infamous conflicts between whites and native Americans, this battle occurred in Montana.
* Some 200 soldiers in the U.S. Army, under General **George Armstrong Custer's** command, were surrounded and killed by between 2,500 and 4,000 Sioux and Cheyenne warriors under the leadership of **Crazy Horse** and **Sitting Bull.**
* These Indians had left their reservation in 1875, although ordered to return by white officials.
* Thereafter, the U.S. Army sought out the Indians and returned them to the Dakotas. Crazy Horse and Sitting Bull accepted life on reservations and were later killed by reservation police.
* This episode was a reaction to the entrance of miners into the Black Hills and to the corrupt behavior of white agents.

Chase of the Nez Perce (1877): Another major conflict occurred in Idaho.
* The **Nez Perce,** a small tribe, refused a U.S. government order to move to a smaller reservation.
* Their leader, **Chief Joseph,** urged them to follow him into Canada.

- The 550 men, women, and children who chose to go were pursued by troops until caught near the Canadian border.
- They were then forced to live in the Indian Territory in Oklahoma, where many soon died of disease and malnutrition.

Wounded Knee, South Dakota (1890): Led by the Seventh Cavalry, this massacre, in which about 200 Sioux Indians died, was the last episode in a year-long effort by whites to stop a Sioux religious revival known as the **Ghost Dance.**

Dawes Severalty Act (1887): Designed to accelerate the assimilation of Native Americans into white culture.
- It provided for the division of Indian lands among individual families and for U.S. citizenship for Native Americans who abandoned tribal allegiances.
- Specifically, 160 acres was allotted to the head of a family, 80 acres to a single adult or an orphan, and 40 acres to each dependent child. Full title to the property was gained after 25 years.
- In actual practice, much of the reservation land was never distributed to individual owners.
- Under this act, nearly on half of the Indian land was lost to white settlement.

Assimilation: In conjunction with the **Dawes Severalty Act,** the Bureau of Indian Affairs also tried other means of assimilation.
- Indian children were taken from their families and sent to white boarding schools.
- Christianity was encouraged, and churches were established on reservations to stop Indian religious festivals.

Theme 2 GROWTH OF INDUSTRY, BUSINESS, AND LABOR

*A*ccelerated industrial expansion took place in America during the final decades of the nineteenth century. The United States had an abundance of raw materials, energy resources, and a cheap labor supply. Technological inventions and entrepreneurial know-how helped to organize large-scale production and distribute manufactured goods to a national market. Freed from the political power of conservative Southern planters, the federal government promoted corporate growth with protective tariffs, along with a new banking and currency system. Public resources were made available for private exploitation along with direct subsidies of land and money.

By 1894, the United States had become the world's leading industrial power. Prosperity was not universally shared, however; the uneven distribution of wealth and the creation of harmful business combinations resulted in problems for workers, farmers, and the middle class, as well as for industrial titans.

INDIVIDUAL KEYS IN THIS THEME

6	Industrial development
7	Evolution of the corporation
8	Ideas about industrial capitalism
9	Workers and the union movement
10	Unions: Action and reaction

Key 6 Industrial development

OVERVIEW *Inventions were critical in fomenting industrial growth. During 1860–90, 440,000 patents were granted, whereas before 1860, only 36,000 patents had been issued. New inventions included the transatlantic telegraph cable, telephone, typewriter, cash register, adding machine, and electric lightbulb. The invention of **new technologies** and the discovery of **new materials** and **production processes** contributed to America's tremendous industrial expansion.*

Henry Bessemer: Developed, during the 1850s in England, the revolutionary **Bessemer process** for producing large quantities of steel by burning out the impurities in molten iron.
- This inexpensive process was independently developed in the United States by **William Kelly** and was largely responsible for making America the world's leading steel producer.
- Together with the **open-hearth process** (which used low-grade ore and scrap metal to produce steel), introduced by **Abram S. Hewitt**, a New Jersey ironmaster, this technology meant that steel could readily be produced for locomotives, steel rails, and the heavy girders used in building construction.

Thomas Edison: An inventor who served as a model for corporate industrial research.
- His inventions, which included the electric lightbulb and the phonograph, became part of American homes.
- Over 1,000 patents were granted to him.

Henry Ford: Revolutionized the automobile industry.
- By 1914, he had introduced the 8-hour day into all his plants, with a minimum wage of $5.00 per day. This "self-made man" was responsible for producing an affordable automobile.
- **The Ford Motor Company** was also partly responsible for making the auto industry a major force in the American economy. Many other industries (e.g., petroleum, construction) began to depend on it for survival.

Frederick Winslow Taylor: Father of **"scientific management."**
- His ideas involved managing human labor efficiently and effectively.

- The science of production, or what became known as **"Taylorism,"** reached its peak during the 1920s, but attempts to bring scientific standards to the performance of workers were central to the growth of American industries in the nineteenth century also.

Railroad expansion: A key component in promoting industrial development.
- As the nation's principal means of transportation, railroads gave industrialists quick and inexpensive access to distant markets and distant sources of raw materials.
- Although railroads existed before the Civil War, railroad trackage grew dramatically after 1860.
- Improvements in technology made travel more efficient and safer.
- Government subsidies encouraged the extension of lines, and railroad development contributed to the growth of the modern corporation—the institution central to late nineteenth-century America.
- Railroad expansion spawned tycoons (e.g., **Cornelius Vanderbilt, James J. Hill**) who acquired control over large railroad empires.

KEY FIGURES

Thomas Edison: Working with a staff of other men in his Menlo Park, New Jersey laboratory, he became a hero to Americans when he invented the lightbulb, phonograph, and motion picture camera and projector, and built power plants that furnished electrical power to urban areas.

Henry Ford: He completed his first automobile in 1893 and had organized the Ford Motor Company by 1903. By 1909 he was producing the first "Model T" car, using the techniques of mass production and the moving assembly line.

Key 7 Evolution of the corporation

OVERVIEW *The corporation became the dominant type of business organization in the post-Civil War period.*

Corporation: A type of business organization that receives a charter from a state government entitling it to certain privileges and immunities. Its evolution enabled entrepreneurs to accumulate vast sums of capital and undertake massive projects.
- Although this type of business organization first evolved in the railroad industry, it soon spread to the steel industry, meat-packing industry, and manufacturing.
- **Investors** buy stock in a corporation and risk only the amount of their investments, called **limited liability.**
- Corporations are also characterized by a set of **managerial techniques,** which include the **division of responsibilities,** a **hierarchy of control, modern cost-accounting procedures,** and a **"middle manager,"** intermediate in status between the workers and the owners.
- Another feature of the modern corporation is **consolidation,** a way to create great industrial organizations.
- Consolidation can be accomplished by **horizontal integration,** thus combining a number of firms involved in the same enterprise into a single corporation.
- More prevalent after 1890 was **vertical integration** which involves taking over the businesses on which a company relies for its primary function.

Andrew Carnegie: A Scottish immigrant who, after working in the railroad industry, opened his own steelworks in Pittsburgh in 1873.
- He bought out rival concerns by controlling the processing of steel from mine to market and by obtaining rebates on his shipments from the railroads so he could cut costs and prices.
- In 1901, he sold his steel interests to the **U.S. Steel Corporation** and devoted the remainder of his life to philanthropy.
  1. He endowed many libraries and contributed to public education.
  2. He also established the **Carnegie Endowment for International Peace** and **Carnegie Hall.**

John D. Rockefeller: A tycoon who, after successfully consolidating the oil industry by 1879, formed the **Standard Oil Trust** in 1882.

- The Standard Oil Trust consisted of 40 corporations that controlled every phase of oil refining.
- The trust was ordered dissolved by Ohio courts in 1892, was then reorganized as a holding company, but was permanently dissolved by a Supreme Court order in 1911.
- Rockefeller retired from active control of the business in that year and devoted his efforts to charity.
  1. The **Rockefeller Institute for Medical Research** was established in 1901, and the **Rockefeller Foundation** in 1913.
  2. By 1937, when Rockefeller died, over $530,000,000 had been given away.

Pools, trusts, and holding companies: Types of business organizations that began to emerge during the 1860s and 1870s.
- In a pool, competing firms agree to divide the market, establish prices, place profits in a common fund, and pro-rate profits. These arrangements, which first emerged in the railroad industry, were also known as **"gentlemen's agreements."**
- Pioneered by the Standard Oil Company in 1882, a *trust* is a form of business combination in which stockholders of affiliated companies turn over their securities and their authority to a board of trustees. The stockholders receive trust certificates and the board of trustees exercises full control of the business.
- During the 1890s, another form of consolidation, the *holding company,* emerged. In this form of business organization, a company owns sufficient stock in other companies and is thus able to dominate their activities. Holding companies made trusts unnecessary and permitted actual mergers.

Impact of corporate evolution: The corporation attempted to eliminate cutthroat competition and business instability.
- What emerged was a system of economic organization that concentrated power in the hands of a few men, bankers such as **J. P. Morgan** and industrial magnets such as **Andrew Carnegie.**
- This concentration of financial power enhanced economic growth, paved the way for large-scale mass production, and stimulated new markets.

KEY FIGURE

John D. Rockefeller: He founded the Standard Oil Company of Ohio in 1870 and had gained control of 90–95 percent of all oil refining in the United States by 1879.

Key 8 Ideas about industrial capitalism

OVERVIEW *The formation of corporations, trusts, and holding companies became a major focus of debate in late nineteenth and early twentieth century America. Because of the disadvantages and problems resulting from industrial expansion, ideologies justifying such economic activity arose.*

Farmers and workers: Criticized the new business philosophy as an attack on America's traditional society. The new economy was eroding their opportunities and stifling their mobility.

Middle-class critics: Noted the corruption in the new industrial enterprises and in politics at all levels. Many businessmen even charged that corporations were not sufficiently modernized and that their methods were inefficient and wasteful.

Big business: Attempted to convince the public that the new corporate economy was compatible with individualism and equal opportunity.

Social Darwinism: The application to society of **Charles Darwin's** laws of **evolution** and **natural selection.**
- Social Darwinism was popularized by several prominent intellectuals of the late nineteenth century.
- According to this theory, if only the fittest organisms survive in the process of natural evolution, in society only the fittest individuals survive in the marketplace.
- Those who attain riches are thus rewarded for their hard work, while those who fail are impoverished by their own shortcomings.
- Over time, society benefits from the triumph of the strong and the talented.
- Social Darwinists believed that economic life was controlled by the natural law of **competition.**
- Social Darwinism coincided with the ideas of **Adam Smith,** particularly in the area of the **law of supply and demand.**
- Although businessmen celebrated the virtues of competition and the free market, as embodied in social Darwinism, they actively sought to eliminate competition and control the free market.

- This ideology had a major impact on American society. **John D. Rockefeller** and **Andrew Carnegie** used it to rationalize their activities, legitimize their success, and confirm their virtues.

William Graham Sumner: Prominent American intellectual who promoted social Darwinism through lectures, articles, and a book entitled *Folkways* (1906).
- He asserted that individuals should have the freedom to struggle to compete and to pursue their self-interests.
- The struggle for survival should not be hampered by laws or by governmental intervention.

Gospel of wealth: A philosophy of business men, usually associated with Andrew Carnegie's book, *The Gospel of Wealth* (1901), which states that wealthy individuals have not only power but also responsibilities; it is their duty to use their wealth to advance social programs. The idea of private wealth as a trust fund for the good of the community encouraged many wealthy industrialists to devote some of their riches to philanthropic enterprises.

Popular literature: Widely read authors included:
- **Russell H. Conwell,** a Baptist minister, fostered the notion of private wealth as something available to all in his **"Acres of Diamonds"** lectures. In stories about people who found opportunities for wealth in their own backyards, Conwell proclaimed that every industrious individual has the chance to get rich.
- **Horatio Alger,** a former minister, wrote over 100 popular novels (e.g., *Sink or Swim, Andy Grant's Pluck*) that proclaimed a similar message: Through work, perseverance, and luck, anyone can become rich.

Critics of Social Darwinism: Not everyone accepted the theory.
- **Lester Frank Ward** argued that human intelligence, not the laws of natural selection, governs civilization. Modern society should use government to intervene in the economy and adjust it to serve human welfare.
- **Henry George,** in his best-seller *Progress and Poverty* (1879), attempted to explain why poverty existed in spite of modern progress.
  1. He pointed to the ability of a few monopolists to gain wealth as a result of rising land values. The value of the land increased because of the growth of society around the land. Such an increase in the value of the land resulting from increased demand was rightfully the property of the community.

2. He thus proposed a **single tax,** replacing all other taxes, which would return this "unearned increment" to the people.
3. Such a tax would distribute wealth more equally, eliminate poverty, and destroy monopolies.
4. **Single-tax societies** developed in many cities as a result of the popularity of his ideas.

- **Edward Bellamy,** in his popular utopian novel, *Looking Backward* (1888), described a new society where want and vice were unknown and happiness prevailed.
  1. Cooperation had replaced competition, and class divisions had disappeared.
  2. A **single trust** controlled by the government conducted all business and equally distributed the resulting economic abundance. Bellamy called his concept "nationalism," which was his brand of socialism.
  3. This novel provided the impetus for the creation of over 160 **Nationalist Clubs,** which promoted Bellamy's ideas.

Key 9   Workers and the union
movement

OVERVIEW *During the last half of the nineteenth century, the industrial work force expanded as industry burgeoned. Poor treatment by management resulted in the formation of organizations to represent the needs of the workers.*

Workers: Workers came primarily from the rural areas of America as well as from all parts of Europe.
- Most immigrants from northern Europe came before 1890, while most of the so-called new immigrants, those from southern and eastern Europe, arrived after 1890.
- New immigrants migrated for employment opportunities as well for escape from poverty and oppression at home.
  1. As new ethnic groups poured into the work force, they encountered Americans of old stock and other ethnics who had arrived earlier.
  2. The various ethnic groups tended to cluster in particular occupations within industries.

Wages and working conditions: Both were poor.
- The average income of the American worker, about $500 per year, was below the minimum required to sustain a reasonable level of comfort.
- Most workers had no job security and labored 10 hours a day at routine, repetitive tasks.
- Workplaces were often unhealthy and unsafe, industrial accidents were frequent, and neither the government nor employers provided workers' compensation.
- Increasing numbers of women and children toiled in factories, earning much lower wages than adult males, to the detriment of their health.
- Labor attempted to improve its status in the workplace by forming **unions,** but unions did not attract most workers and won few gains against the titans of industry.

Knights of Labor: Founded in 1869 by **Uriah S. Stephens** as the first national labor organization.

- It started as a secret organization whose membership was open to both skilled and unskilled workers; only lawyers, bankers, liquor dealers, and professional gamblers were excluded.
- It supported an 8-hour day, equal pay for equal work, better wages, abolition of child labor, safety and health laws, arbitration of labor disputes, prohibition of foreign contract labor, workers' cooperative associations, a graduated income tax, and government ownership of railroads and other public utilities.
- After 1879, under **Terence V. Powderly,** the order expanded, reaching a membership of over 700,000 by 1886.
- As local unions or assemblies launched strikes against Powderly's wishes after 1885, the union declined. By 1890 membership had shrunk to 100,000, and thereafter the organization disappeared.

American Federation of Labor (AFL): Created in 1881 by **Samuel Gompers** and consisted of many separate, skilled craft unions.

- Was opposed to organizing women and unskilled workers, thereby excluding about 90 percent of American labor.
- Supported higher wages, improved working conditions, an 8-hour day, use of union-made products, and passage of state and federal legislation to benefit labor.
- Claimed about 500,000 members by 1900.
- Advocated collective bargaining, but supported the strike if needed.

Industrial Workers of the World (IWW, Wobblies): Organized in 1905 under the leadership of **"Big Bill" Haywood.**

- Organized unskilled industrial workers, such as Western miners and lumbermen, and advocated militant agitation, willful obstruction of industry, and damage to businesses in case of disputes.
- Aimed to create a single, united labor organization made up of all trades, skill levels, and races.
- Sought to build a new, voluntary, cooperative human society.
- Never had more than about 60,000 members; after 1913, its membership declined.

Key 10 Unions: Action and reaction

OVERVIEW *The union movement used the strike as a weapon but was thwarted by management, with government support.*

Railroad Strike of 1877: The first major strike, which began against the **B&O Railroad Company,** but spread to other lines in the Eastern states and some areas west of the Mississippi.
- Protesting a 10 percent wage cut, railroad workers called a strike and stopped railroads from operating.
- To quell riots in Pennsylvania, Maryland, West Virginia, and Illinois, federal troops were employed.
- Before the strike was broken, $5 million worth of property was destroyed.
- Railroad workers went back to work at lower wages set by the railroads.

Haymarket Riot (1886): So named because it took place in **Haymarket Square** in Chicago on May 4, 1886.
- This event followed a nationwide strike for an 8-hour day, sponsored by the **AFL** and some local units of the **Knights of Labor;** therefore they became identified with the episode.
- Sympathetic anarchists were addressing a protest meeting in Haymarket Square, held by the strikers.
- During the meeting, a bomb exploded in the midst of police; seven died and many others were wounded.
- Eight anarchists were convicted of murder as a result.

Homestead Strike (1892): One of the most violent strikes in America occurred when the **Carnegie Steel Company** announced pay cuts for unionized members of the **Amalgamated Association of Iron and Steel Workers,** an AFL affiliate.
- Seven lives were lost when 300 Pinkerton detectives were brought to the plant so that strikebreakers could be hired.
- A pitched battle broke out on July 6, 1892, and the Pinkertons finally surrendered.
- Plant manager **Henry C. Frick** and local law officials then requested militia protection, so the Pennsylvania governor sent the state's National Guard, some 8,000 troops, to Homestead to restore order and protect strikebreakers.

- A radical anarchist named **Alexander Beckman** wounded Henry C. Frick in an attempted assassination.
- Four months after the strike began, the union finally surrendered.
- By 1900, Amalgamated's membership had shrunk to fewer than 7,000, from 24,000 in 1891.

Pullman Strike (1894): A strike by **Pullman Palace Car Company** workers protesting a 25 percent reduction in wages and over policies in the company town near Chicago.
- Led by its president, **Eugene V. Debs,** the **American Railway Union** aided strikers by extending a boycott of Pullman cars to 27 states, paralyzing transportation from Chicago to the Pacific coast.
- Illinois Governor **John P. Altgeld** would not call out the militia to protect employers, but over his objections President Cleveland sent 2,000 troops to restore order and protect the U.S. mails.
- Then Attorney General **Richard Olney** obtained an **injunction** forbidding interference with the mail and interstate commerce.
  1. It virtually forbade Debs and his associates to continue the strike.
  2. Ignoring the injunction, they were arrested, tried for contempt of court, and sentenced to 6 months in prison.
- With the union leaders in jail, the strike ended.
- After the strike, the injunction became a powerful weapon for employers to use against strikers.

Theme 3 CITY LIFE AND THE IMPACT OF INDUSTRIALIZATION

*I*n the post–Civil War period, American cities became centers of economic, social, and cultural life. Industrialization, expansion of commerce, and new social and cultural values gradually extended their influence to the entire nation. The cities embodied new technology and industry, along with conditions that fostered misgovernment, poverty, traffic jams, overcrowding, filth, epidemics, and natural disasters.

INDIVIDUAL KEYS IN THIS THEME

11	Urban development
12	The immigrant
13	Popular culture
14	Intellectual and elite culture

Key 11 Urban development

OVERVIEW *One of the most significant developments of the late nineteenth century was the great movement of rural people from the United States and Europe to America's business and industrial centers. Cities offered entertainment, conveniences, culture, educational institutions, and, most importantly, employment.*

Urban growth: From 1860 to 1910, America's urban population increased sevenfold.
- The 1920 census revealed that, for the first time, most Americans lived in urban areas of 2,500 inhabitants or more.
- Urban growth resulted primarily from southern and eastern European immigration.
- Also, a substantial number of blacks moved from the rural South to industrial cities during the 1880s and 1890s.
- Large urban areas contained a variety of ethnic groups.

Urban transportation: Urban growth stimulated the need for better transportation.
- Wooden blocks, bricks, or asphalt were now used to pave streets.
- In 1870 New York opened its first elevated railway, and Richmond, Virginia, introduced the electric trolley line in 1888.
- The first American subway was opened in 1897 in Boston.
- **John A. Roebling's** steel-cable suspension span, the **Brooklyn Bridge,** was completed in the 1880s.

Urban politics: Although its size and structure varied from city to city, the urban **political machine** arose to fill the power vacuum that the rapid growth of cities had created.
- The political machine was also a product of the potential voting power of large immigrant communities.
- A machine consisted of a group of urban **"bosses"** whose goal was to win votes for their political organization.
- A boss utilized many approaches to win and ensure support. He might provide food or fuel to individuals in need and often found jobs for the unemployed or cut through red tape to remedy neighborhood or individual problems.
- Machine supporters were usually rewarded with jobs in city government, in city agencies, or in the transit system, as well as with the chance to rise in the political organization itself.

- Through **graft** and **corruption,** machines were also vehicles for making money.
- New York City's **Tammany Hall,** with **William M. Tweed** as its boss, was a notorious example.
- Positive achievements of the political machine included modernizing city **infrastructures,** expanding the role of government, and establishing stability.
- Machines forged important economic relationships with local businesses and exhibited skill in winning elections and in retaining voters' loyalties.

Key 12 The immigrant

OVERVIEW *Urban centers became havens for ethnic groups. Although their labor was essential for America's growing industrial economy, many of them faced discrimination.*

City dwellers and city life: Most immigrants settled in ethnic communities within cities. Individuals from the same province, town or village could often be found in a particular ethnic neighborhood.
- The city exhibited great contrasts in living conditions, from palatial mansions to slums.
- Rural, unskilled immigrants generally inhabited decaying or makeshift housing where the average population density was high.
- So-called **immigrant ghettos** provided cultural cohesiveness, eased the pain of separation from the native land, and eased the adjustment to American city life.
- These areas provided ethnic newspapers and theaters and native foods, as well as church and fraternal organizations, that served as links to former homelands.

Americanization: In their desire to become Americans, immigrants discovered that ethnicity had to compete with **assimilation.**
- American institutions (e.g., schools, stores, and churches) encouraged assimilation.
- The first stage on the road to becoming an American usually involved **discrimination** by native-born Americans.
- Immigrants were excluded from better residential areas, received little protection in employment, and endured biased remarks regarding their ethnicity.
- Over time, immigrants adapted to American culture.
  1. **Acculturation** included learning English and gaining an understanding of the American legal system and government and its customs and traditions.
  2. This stage of assimilation usually occurred among second- or even third-generation descendants of immigrants.

Nativism: This fear of foreigners was acted out in a variety of ways.
- Immigrants were **discriminated** against because of differences in race, religion, and political beliefs, and because of economic fears that they posed a threat to native-born American workers.

- New organizations arose in response to these fears. In 1887 a self-educated lawyer, **Henry Bowers,** founded the **Protective Association,** an anti-Catholic group whose aim was to stop immigration. Its membership reached 500,000 by 1894.
- That same year the **Immigration Restriction League** was established in Boston by five Harvard alumni. It advocated the use of **literacy tests** and other means to screen immigrants.

Key 13 Popular culture

OVERVIEW *A unique **middle class,** with its own **culture,** began to influence American life. Its growth and increasing prosperity resulted from the rise of American industry. This middle class constituted the primary market for consumer goods.*

Mass consumption: The new consumer market resulted in the development of affordable products and new merchandising techniques.
- The ready-made garment industry expanded to clothe almost all Americans.
- By 1900, Americans had learned to buy and prepare food differently because canned foods and refrigeration were available.
- Chain stores such as **A&P** and **F. W. Woolworth** made their debut. The growth of the mail-order business also began with the **Sears-Roebuck** catalog.

Improved quality of life: Because of increased purchasing power and better diet, middle-class Americans began to enjoy a higher quality of life.
- Their general health improved, and they had longer life expectancies.
- Leisure time increased, particularly for members of the urban middle and professional classes.
- New forms of recreation and entertainment became available.

Sports: There was an interest in sports, and organized spectator sports became popular.
- By the early twentieth century, baseball had become both an important business and the national pastime.
- Other sports (e.g., football, basketball, golf, tennis, bicycling, boxing) became popular as well.

Popular culture: Aside from sports, other types of entertainment arose to satisfy American tastes.
- These included the **musical comedy, vaudeville, circuses, Wild West shows,** and, most important, the **movies.** Motion pictures attracted mass audiences in all areas of the United States.
- **Reading** also became an increasingly popular pastime.
  1. So-called **dime novels** were popular; their subject matter included adventure and romance.

2. The circulation of newspapers increased almost nine times from 1870 to 1910.
3. **Newspaper chains** and **national press services** emerged which standardized the presentation of news across the nation.
4. Introduced by publisher **Joseph Pulitzer** and popularized by newspaper chain owner **William Randolph Hearst, yellow journalism,** a sensational style of reporting, emphasized scandals and exposes, sports, fashion, and popular entertainment, in order to sell papers.
5. Many popular **magazines,** such as *McClure's Magazine,* inexpensively priced and geared to a mass audience, also appeared.

Key 14 Intellectual and elite culture

OVERVIEW *During the late nineteenth century, a new cultural and intellectual life, influenced by the growth of industry and the rise of the city, was developing among the upper classes and intellectuals.*

Writers: Stephen Crane, Upton Sinclair, Frank Norris, and **Theodore Dreiser** probed the problems created by an urban-industrial society.

Art: By the turn of the century, most major American cities had museums or art galleries where both American and European art could be viewed. A number of truly American artists emerged at this time as well.
- **Winslow Homer** painted New England maritime life, while **James McNeel Whistler** introduced Oriental concepts into American art.
- Reflecting the new urban industrial society were members of the so-called **ashcan school,** which captured the social realities of that time. **John Sloan** painted American urban slums, while **Edward Hopper** focused on the aspects of the modern city.

Darwinism: The **theory of evolution,** associated with English scientist **Charles Darwin,** had a profound intellectual impact.
- The theory states that human evolved from earlier life forms (most recently, creatures similar to apes) through a process of natural selection.
- This theory was widely accepted by most urban professionals and the educated classes. It won acceptance in colleges and schools and even among most middle class Protestant religious leaders.
- Strong opposition to this theory remained among rural Americans who were wedded to fundamentalist religious beliefs and older values.
- Darwin's ideas created a split between the **cosmopolitan culture of the city** and the **provincial culture of rural areas.**

Pragmatism: This philosophical movement accepted the idea of organic evolution, but also asserted that modern society should be guided by scientific inquiry, not by inherited ideals and moral principles.
- In other words, an idea or institution is valid if it can be demonstrated to work.
- Exponents of pragmatism included **William James, Charles S. Pierce,** and **John Dewey.** Dewey, for instance, advocated an

education in which students would acquire knowledge that would help them deal with life.

Scientific inquiry: This spirit permeated intellectual thought.

- **Economists** such as **Richard T. Ely** argued for a more pragmatic use of the discipline.
- **Sociologists** (e.g., **Edward A. Ross** and **Lester F. Ward**) advocated use of the scientific method in tackling social and political problems.
- **Progressive historians** such as **Charles A. Beard** asserted that economic factors had been most influential in historical development.

Education: Urban-industrial society emphasized specialized skills and scientific knowledge to prepare American workers. The educational system responded.

- **Free public education** spread; by 1900, 31 states had compulsory attendance laws.
- The **Morrill Land Grant Act** of 1862 enabled 69 land-grant institutions of higher education to be established.
- In addition to the federal government's efforts, business titans endowed private colleges and universities.
- Following Harvard's lead, other colleges and universities adopted the **elective system of course selection** and began to offer modern language, fine arts, and physical and social science courses.
- Improved **technical training** became available in law, medicine, architecture, engineering, journalism, business, and education.
- Graduate education grew, and educational opportunities for women expanded as well with the growing number of women's colleges.

Theme 4 GILDED AGE POLITICS

*T*he growth of monopolies, the conflict between labor and management, the decline of the agrarian economy, and a financial system that produced a major collapse about every 20 years—all these had an impact on American political institutions. Nevertheless, because social and economic conditions were changing faster than ideas about public policy, the American political system in the 1880s and 1890s remained locked in a rigid stalemate. The two parties appeared practically identical, and neither exerted leadership.

Key 15 The nature of American politics

OVERVIEW *Popular enthusiasms for party politics had little connection with the government's actions. Americans were politically active, because of broad regional, ethnic, or religious sentiments, with little regard for the issues.*

The party system: Characterized by stability, loyalty, and high voter turnout.
- Both the Democratic and Republican parties were pro-business and were opposed to economic radicalism.
- Both advocated a "sound currency" and the existing financial system.
- Republicans tended to be more nativist and to advocate legislation favoring temperance and restricting immigration.
- The federal government and for the most part, state and local governments were expected to do very little.

Congress and the electorate: The popular vote was divided almost evenly between Republicans and Democrats.
- In Congress, the **Republicans** dominated the Senate, while the **Democrats** generally controlled the House.
- **Voter turnout** for presidential elections averaged over 78 percent of all eligible voters, while the turnout ranged from 60 to 80 percent in nonpresidential years.
- **Party loyalties** were determined by region, as well as religious and ethnic differences.
  1. Cultural inclinations and prejudices, rather than economic interest, determined party identification.
  2. Such identification was of central importance.

The campaign: Political campaigns were important public events akin to spectator sports and mass popular entertainment today.
- Political organizations provided social and cultural functions to promote party loyalty and voter turnout.
- Parties were primarily concerned with winning elections and controlling patronage, rather than with issues.
- Party bosses and machines took center stage in every campaign.

Stalwarts: Term first used by a group of Republicans who supported Grant for a third term against Garfield.

- Stalwarts were active during the Hayes administration.
- Leaders of this group included **Roscoe Conkling** (1867–1881), a New York senator and leader of the Republican Party in New York, and **Simon Cameron.**

Half-breeds: Term (used mostly after the election of President **Rutherford B. Hayes**) referring to a section of the Republican Party.

- Half-breeds supported civil service reform and opposed corruption in government.
- They were led by **James G. Blaine.**

Mugwumps: Term (first used in the presidential election of 1884) referring to a group of Republicans who withdrew from the party in protest at the nomination of James G. Blaine and gave their support to **Grover Cleveland,** the Democratic candidate.

Key 16 Gilded Age presidents

OVERVIEW *In the late nineteenth century, the **Republican** and **Democratic parties** enjoyed a strength and stability unmatched since then. Governments lacked agencies and the will to perform any significant role in American economic life. In addition, American politics lacked an ideology sufficient to justify any major expansion of government responsibilities.*

Rutherford B. Hayes (1877–81): Because the 1876 presidential election was disputed, Rutherford B. Hayes, the winner, was referred to by critics as **"His Fraudulency."**
- His presidency was undistinguished because the competitive party system left him with little opportunity for independent leadership.
- He had little success in promoting a national civil service system.
- However, he did secure a victory for civil service in the New York **Customs House dispute.**
  1. In 1877 he dismissed **Chester A. Arthur** and **Alonzo B. Cornell** from their positions as officials of the Customs House when they refused to carry out civil service reform measures.
  2. New York Senator Roscoe Conkling had been using the Customs House for political patronage and opposed the dismissals.
  3. President Hayes received Senate approval for his appointees to replace the dismissed officials in spite of Conkling's opposition.
- Hayes's effectiveness was further hampered by his early announcement that he would not seek reelection.

James A. Garfield (1881): A self-made man and former congressman from Ohio, James A. Garfield was the victorious dark horse candidate in the 1880 presidential election against Democrat General **Winfield Scott Hancock.**
- As president, his appointment of a collector for the Port of New York over the protests of Senators **Conkling** and **Platt** led to their resignation from the Senate.
- Garfield supported civil service reform but had accomplished little by July 2, 1881, when he was shot in the Pennsylvania Railroad Station in Washington, D.C., by **Charles J. Guiteau,** a disappointed office seeker; Garfield died 2 months later.

Chester A. Arthur (1881–85): Vice president under Garfield, Chester A. Arthur had been an ally of Republican political boss Roscoe Conkling of New York and a supporter of the traditional spoils system.

- However, as president, he urged Congress to enact a civil service law, which was passed in 1883.
- Other significant events of his presidency were the **Chinese Exclusion Act (1882)** and the **Immigration Act (1882).**

Grover Cleveland (1885–89, 1893–97): A reform governor of New York (1883–85), Democrat Grover Cleveland became president in 1885.

- He exhibited a commitment to economy in government.
- He believed in a very limited role for the federal government in regard to social problems.
- He supported civil service reform and a lower tariff but was not successful in getting Congress to lower tariffs in 1887.
- Although defeated by Republican **Benjamin Harrison** in the 1888 election, Cleveland again became president in 1893. Benjamin Harrison was again the Republican nominee, and **James B. Weaver** was the candidate of the **People's Party,** a new third party.
- Cleveland's second term was similarly devoted to minimal government and hostility to government involvement in economic or social problems. Despite his opposition, the **Wilson-Gorman Tariff Act** was passed in 1894.
- Significant *first administration* events: the **Haymarket Riot (1886),** the **Interstate Commerce Act (1887),** the creation of a **new cabinet position: Secretary of Agriculture (1889).**
- Significant *second administration* events: the **panic of 1893, repeal of the Sherman Silver Purchase Act (1893), Coxey's Army (1894),** the **Pullman Strike (1894).**

Benjamin Harrison (1889–93): Benjamin Harrison was the grandson of President **William Henry Harrison** and a Republican senator from Indiana.

- In 1888 he defeated Grover Cleveland despite having fewer popular votes.
- Main events of his administration: **McKinley Tariff Act (1890); Sherman Silver Purchase Act (1890); Disability Pension Act (1890); admission of six states to the Union (1889–1890); the first Pan-American Conference (1889).**

Key 17 National issues

OVERVIEW *Although the Democratic and Republican parties did not take distinctively different positions on important public issues, national issues emerged nevertheless. They included* **currency,** *the* **tariff, immigration, civil service, presidential succession,** *the* **railroads,** *and the* **trusts.**

Bland-Allison Act (1878): Directed the U.S. Treasury to purchase between $2 million and $4 million worth of silver each month to be coined into silver dollars.
- In 1873, Congress had withdrawn silver from the coinage list, and this action was blamed for a contraction of the currency.
- The purpose of the act was to maintain a higher price for silver and to strengthen declining farm prices and industrial wages, by increasing the volume of money in circulation.
- The Bland-Allison Act provided for an international monetary conference that was held but produced no significant results.

Tariff Commission of 1882/Tariff of 1883: Because of popular demand for tariff reform, Congress established the commission in 1882.
- It recommended that the tariff rates be reduced by no less than 20 percent.
- The tariff of 1883 lowered some duties and raised others; the overall result was a 5 percent reduction.

Immigration Act of 1882: Prohibited the immigration of criminals, paupers, the insane, and other persons likely to become public charges and levied a head tax of 50 cents on each immigrant.

Chinese Exclusion Act (1882): Initially passed in 1882; extended in 1892 and in 1902.
- The entry of Chinese laborers into the United States was prohibited for a 10-year period.
- The act was extended for 10 years in 1892 and then extended indefinitely in 1902.
- The law was repealed in 1943.

Pendleton Act (1883): Created a **Civil Service Commission** of three members, to be appointed by the president.
- The commission was authorized to establish and administer a competitive examination to determine, on a merit basis, the fitness of civil service employees.

- A list of offices was set up for merit appointments.
- Political assessments of federal office holders and removal because of failure to make voluntary contributions were prohibited.

Presidential Succession Act (1886): Provided for succession to the U.S. presidency in the event of the death, removal, resignation, or inability of the president or vice president. The order of succession was to fall to the heads of the executive departments in the order of the establishment of those departments.

Interstate Commerce Act (1887): Set up a five person agency, the **Interstate Commerce Commission (ICC),** which required that railroads post rates publicly and that rates be reasonable and just.
- Pooling and rebates were declared illegal.
- The act also prohibited long-haul versus short-haul discrimination, and mandated that complaints against railroads be investigated.
- The law proved ineffective because the first chairman of the ICC favored the railroads and subsequent Supreme Court decisions weakened the ICC's authority.

Hatch Act (1887): Provided a federal subsidy for each state and territory to be used for the creation of agricultural experiment stations. Its purpose was to encourage agricultural research and assist farmers.

Omnibus Bill of 1889: Admitted four new states to the Union: North Dakota, South Dakota, Washington, and Montana.

Sherman Antitrust Act (1890): Prohibited monopolies by declaring any business combination "in restraint of trade" illegal.
- It was circumvented by corporations, which formed holding companies.
- The courts failed to enforce the act.

McKinley Tariff Act (1890): An unpopular law; raised the tariff on many items, resulting in an average duty of 49.5 percent.
- Placed new duties on agricultural items.
- Discontinued the duty on raw sugar and provided a bounty of 2 cents per pound on domestic sugar.

Disability Pension Act (1890): Provided pensions for all Union veterans who had served at least 90 days and were now unable to perform manual labor, regardless of origin of disability.
- From 1891 to 1895 the number of pensioners increased from 676,000 to 970,000.
- During the same period the cost rose from $81 million to $135 million.

Sherman Silver Purchase Act (1890): Designed to halt a decline in the price of silver and to improve economic conditions.
- It provided for the purchase by the U.S. Treasury of 4.5 million ounces of silver each month.
- The silver was to be paid for in treasury notes redeemable in gold.
- The law was repealed in 1893.

Pan-American Conference (1889–90): Held in Washington, D.C., with representatives from 18 American nations, it established an **International Bureau of American Republics (Pan-American Union)** and prepared the way for tariff reciprocity.

Wilson-Gorman Tariff Act (1894): Lowered duties as much as 10 percent on average. Raw wool, lumber, and copper were placed on the free list.
- Reduced rates on other items but replaced the duty on sugar, which had been eliminated in 1890.
- Also provided for a 2 percent tax on incomes over $4000, a provision held to be unconstitutional in 1895.
- Became law without President Cleveland's signature.

Key 18 Agrarian unrest

OVERVIEW *As an urban-industrial society began to dominate the American scene, farmers suffering economic decline became concerned with the problems of the modern economy. Eager for government assistance, they formed a political protest movement known as* ***populism.***

Agrarian malaise: During the last half of the nineteenth century, farmers believed that the new urban industrial society, which no longer valued the traditional virtues of rural life, was dominating American life.
- This agrarian malaise was a result of economic complaints, an outgrowth of the isolation of farm life, and a reaction to the departure of increasing numbers of young people who left the farms for the cities.
- The discontent contributed to the creation of the **Populist Party** in the 1890s.
- Agrarian malaise found an outlet in the **literature** of this period. Representative of the writers who chronicled the trials of rural life was **Hamlin Garland.**

Grange movement: Various activities that resulted in the formation of farmers' organizations in the post–Civil War years culminated in 1867 with the establishment of the **National Grange of the Patrons of Husbandry.**
- Founded by **Oliver H. Kelley,** a clerk in the U.S. Department of Agriculture, for the promotion of agriculture, the Grange movement acquainted farmers with new scientific agricultural techniques.
- It also attempted to promote socialization and a sense of community among farmers.
- Following the depression of 1873, membership grew and local chapters focused on political goals.
  1. They urged political action to curb monopolistic practices of the railroads and warehouses.
  2. They sought to subject railroads to government controls.
- They also set up cooperative stores, creameries, elevators, warehouses, insurance companies, and factories.
- During the 1870s, Grangers held the political balance in several Midwestern states.
  1. **Granger laws** were passed in four states to regulate railroad rates and the practices of elevator owners.
  2. However, these regulations were soon disallowed by the courts.

- Founded in 1872, **Montgomery Ward and Company,** the first mail-order business, emerged specifically to meet the needs of Grangers.
- By the late 1870s, the Grange movement began to lose strength. The return of agrarian prosperity and the political inexperience of many Grange leaders contributed to the movement's decline.

Farmers' Alliances: Before the Grange movement had faded, the first Farmers' Alliance was created in 1873. These alliances had several goals:
- Promoted social gatherings and attempted to improve education through lectures and the circulation of books.
- Sought to organize farmers against railroad abuses, industrial monopolies, and currency controls.
- Formed cooperatives and established stores, banks, and processing plants.
- Stressed cooperation among farmers and were notable for the prominent role played by women.
- In the late 1880s, exerted political pressure on the local and national levels by working through the Democratic Party and then by forming the People's or Populist party.

Populist Party: Formed in 1891 through the efforts of Farmers' Alliances, the Populist Party took an active part in the presidential elections of 1892, 1896, 1900, 1904, and 1908.
- It supported free and unlimited coinage of silver, government ownership of railroads, telegraphs and telephone lines, a graduated income tax, direct election of U.S. senators, postal savings banks, and the use of the **initiative, referendum,** and **recall.**
- **James B. Weaver,** the Populist candidate, received 22 electoral votes and more than 1 million popular votes in the 1892 presidential election.
  1. It failed to receive the expected support from labor.
  2. Its political objectives were taken over by the two major parties.
  3. Support by farmers declined as their situation improved in the late 1890s.

Key 19 Crisis in the 1890s

OVERVIEW *The 1890s was a tense and gloomy decade. A severe depression began in 1893; labor unrest and violence climaxed in the strikes of 1894 (see Key 10).*

Rigidity and proposals for change: During this time of national crisis:
- Grover Cleveland's rigid conservatism exemplified the continuing failure of both major political parties to respond to the nation's problems.
- The Populist Party, with its proposals to reform the American political system, emerged.

Panic of 1893: The causes of this depression, which was unprecedented in its severity and its persistence, included **agricultural depression, decline of the U.S. gold reserve,** and **unsound railroad financing.**
- The panic began in March 1893 when the Philadelphia and Reading Railroad declared bankruptcy and the gold reserve (the amount of gold held in the U.S. Treasury as backing for paper currency in circulation) dropped below $100,000,000.
- The effects spread rapidly as banks failed, a number of railroad companies went into receivership, and strikes, unemployment, and violence became widespread.
- About 20 percent of the labor force was out of work, the highest level of unemployment in American history up to that time.
- Real prosperity did not return until 1901.

Coxey's army: Following the panic of 1893, **Jacob S. Coxey**, an Ohio businessman and Populist, advocated a federally sponsored public works program as a way to put the unemployed to work, and also supported inflation of the currency.
- Disgusted with Congress's lack of action regarding his proposals, Coxey organized a group of about 500 unemployed persons, who marched to Washington, D.C. in 1894 from Masillon, Ohio, demanding that Congress issue $500 million in fiat money to provide jobs for the unemployed in constructing roads.
- Armed police barred the marchers from the Capitol, and Coxey was arrested and later convicted of walking on the grass.
- The protest failed to prod Congress into action.

Silver issue: Because the financial panic had weakened the government's monetary system, the "money question," or currency issue, assumed center stage.

- Silver was central to this conflict.
- Gold and silver had been recognized as a basis for the dollar, but by the 1870s the **remonetization** (restoration to use as legal tender) of silver had taken place.
- By the 1890s, silver mine owners were eager to have the government purchase their surplus silver for much more than the market price.
- Discontented farmers wanted an inflation of the currency to raise the prices of farm products and ease payment of their debts.
- They demanded **free and unlimited coinage of silver** at the old ratio of 16 to 1.
- Under the 1890 **Sherman Silver Purchase Act**, however, the silver purchased from the mine owners was not to be coined, so the amount of money in circulation did not increase materially, and the price of silver kept falling.
- Convinced that the Sherman Silver Purchase Act was responsible for draining gold from the U.S. Treasury, President Cleveland called Congress into special session and demanded the repeal of the act.
- Congress supported his recommendation, but in the process southern and western Democrats spilt from Cleveland's eastern followers.
- In short, silver was viewed by its supporters as a panacea that could eliminate the indebtedness of whole regions of the nation.

Key 20 Election of 1896

OVERVIEW *The money question became a major issue in the 1896 election.*

The Populist appeal: The money question surfaced with the Populists for tactical reasons.
- Populists needed money to finance their campaign, and silver mine owners were willing to support it, provided the silver issue assumed center stage.
- The money question was also viewed as a way for Populists to appeal to those not engaged in farming.

Election of 1896: The two candidates had opposite campaign styles and views on the money question.
- The victorious Republican candidate, **William McKinley,** polled 51.1 percent of the popular vote.
  1. He conducted a "front porch" campaign from his home in Canton, Ohio.
  2. He advocated sound money (the gold standard).
- **William Jennings Bryan,** the candidate of the Democrats and the Populists, received 47.7 percent of the popular vote.
  1. He campaigned extensively, traveling 18,000 miles and addressing about 5 million Americans.
  2. He supported the unlimited coinage of silver.
- Rising farm prices due to overseas crop failures helped to assure a Republican victory.

William McKinley: A former congressman (1877–83, 1885–91) and governor of Ohio (1892–96), he served as president from 1897 to 1901.
- His Republican administration brought a tariff increase, the gold standard, and prosperity.
- It also initiated the era of overseas imperialism with the Spanish-American War (1898), the annexation of Hawaii (1899), and the open-door policy (1899).
- McKinley was shot by **Leon Czolgosz,** an anarchist, on September 6, 1901, while at the Pan-American Exposition in Buffalo, New York.
- He died shortly thereafter, whereupon Vice President Theodore Roosevelt assumed the presidency.

Dingley Tariff Act (1897): Raised tariff rates to a new high average of 57 percent.

- It restored the principle of reciprocity, imposed high duties on wool and hides, and listed duties on over 2,000 items.
- Until 1909, the act remained virtually unchanged.

Gold Standard Act of 1900: Confirmed the commitment to the gold standard.

- The gold dollar of 25.8 grains became the standard unit of value. Other forms of U.S. money were placed on parity with it.
- A gold reserve of $150,000,000 was established for redemption of paper currency.
- The act also allowed banks with small amounts of capital to be chartered in small towns.

Aftermath: By 1900, farmers' economic status had improved and the industrial development of the United States continued to increase. In consequence:

- The money crisis had faded.
- The Populists began to disappear as a political power.

KEY QUOTATION

You shall not press down upon the brow of labor this crown of thorns; you shall not crucify mankind upon a cross of gold.

William Jennings Bryan
"Cross of Gold" speech, delivered at the
Democratic Presidential Convention, 1896

Theme 5 THE PROGRESSIVE ERA: REFORM IN AMERICA

*T*he turn of the century was characterized by reform. This so-called **Progressive Era** saw a series of movements aimed at renovating or restoring American society, its values and its institutions. These efforts were a response to the economic, social, and political development of the time.

Industrialization, rapidly growing cities, mass immigration to America, and the depression of the 1890s created disorder and fostered inefficiency in the United States. While the reform movements and those who participated in them were not always clearly definable as Progressive, Progressive reformers did share certain common ideas.

INDIVIDUAL KEYS IN THIS THEME

21	Who were the Progressives?
22	Governmental and legislative reform
23	Social and economic reform
24	Roosevelt's Square Deal administration
25	Roosevelt's conservation policies
26	Taft as successor
27	Wilson's New Freedom administration

Key 21 Who were the Progressives?

OVERVIEW *Historians have not been able to definitively agree on this question. In general, the individuals and organizations that espoused Progressive beliefs existed in all levels of society, although a new middle class of professional men and women formed the vanguard of reform.*

Progressive beliefs: Progressive reformers believed that the laissez-faire system was obsolete, yet realized that a radical shift away from capitalism was dangerous. In general, they:
- Sought to end abuses of power in America (e.g., by monopolies and government).
- Believed in the idea of progress—the growth and advancement of the United States.
- Believed that reformed institutions would replace corrupt power.
- Would apply principles of science and efficiency to all economic, social, and political institutions.
- Viewed government as a key player in creating an orderly, stable, and improved society.
- Believed that the government had the power to combat special interests and work for the good of the community, state, or nation.

Social Gospel movement: This powerful religious crusade emphasized **social responsibility** as a means to salvation.
- Its followers believed that church-based inspiration and humanitarian work could transform society, particularly in U.S. cities.
- As part of the Progressive movement, its spokesmen included **Walter Rauschenbusch,** a Protestant theologian with socialist inclinations, who wrote about human salvation through Christian reform.
- The **Salvation Army,** which offers material and spiritual services to the urban poor, is an example of the Social Gospel movement in action.

Muckrakers: These crusading writers of books and magazine articles exposed graft, corruption, and dishonesty in business.
- The word *muckrakers,* coined by **Theodore Roosevelt,** alluded to a character in **John Bunyan's** *Pilgrim's Progress* who rejected a crown for a muckrake, that is, a rake used to gather dung into a pile.
- Muckrakers attacked the social ills of the age (e.g., slums, prostitution, delinquency).

- Examples of muckrakers include: **Ida M. Tarbell,** who exposed corruption in the Standard Oil Company; **Lincoln Steffens,** who wrote *Shame of the Cities,* **Jacob Riis,** a Danish immigrant and New York newspaper reporter who exposed the conditions in tenement houses; and **Upton Sinclair,** who wrote about the meat-packing industry in Chicago.
- Because of mass-circulation newspapers and magazines, the work of muckrakers had a major impact on American society.

Settlement house movement: This movement sought to improve the lives of slum dwellers by helping them to obtain more education, appreciation of the arts, improved housing, and better jobs.

- Located in slum neighborhoods and run by educated, middle-class women, settlement houses offered immigrant families assistance in adjusting to American life.
- Although settlement house workers refrained from condemning the lifestyles of slum dwellers, they did impart their own middle-class values to neighborhood residents through their services.
- These houses became a training ground for women leaders and launched the social work profession in America.
  1. Through her experiences at **Hull House,** social worker **Jane Addams** became politically involved in Chicago in order to "clean up" the neighborhood.
  2. She chronicled her ideas and experiences as a leading reformer in *Twenty Years at Hull House* (1910).

Professionals: These new middle-class workers derived their status from their educational and individual accomplishments, not from family background.

- By the end of the nineteenth century, they were organizing their professions by forming associations.
- Their aim was to restrict entry into the professions by establishing rigorous standards for new members and excluding the untrained, incompetent, and undesirable.
- As Progressive reformers, they advocated the use of scientific techniques in reforming American society.
- At this time, women began to enter the professions in small numbers.
  1. They were concentrated in "domestic" professions such as teaching, nursing, and (later) social work.
  2. They created professional organizations such as The **National Education Association (1905)** and set admission standards.

Women's associations: The **women's club movement** played a leading role in Progressive social reforms.

- Although initially concerned with literary and educational activities, these groups changed their focus to social betterment.
- The middle- and upper-class memberships extended their influence beyond the home and the family by supporting social legislation, particularly laws regarding the labor of women and children.
- They often joined with other women's groups to further a cause.

Legacy: The legacy of the Progressive movement is evident in the legislation passed during the 1920s and, more importantly, during the New Deal era of the 1930s. Progressive ideas about child labor, for example, as well as the Progressive belief in the power of the federal government as an advocate for the oppressed, can be seen in the laws of those later years.

KEY FIGURES

Jane Addams: She founded (1899) America's most famous settlement house, **Hull House,** which became the model for more than 400 other settlement houses in the United States.

Jacob Riis: In his book *How the Other Half Lives* (1890), he described the tenements of the time as practically sunless and airless, so that dwellers and visitors were nearly "poisoned" by the smells.

Upton Sinclair: In his novel *The Jungle* (1906) he wrote about the unsafe and unsanitary conditions in the meat-packing industry, leading to the passage of the **Meat Inspection Act.**

Key 22 Governmental and legislative reform

OVERVIEW *A principal goal of the Progressives, in their quest for order and justice, was to streamline American political institutions.*

Political parties and reform: Political parties were singled out as being corrupt, undemocratic, outmoded, and inefficient, so energy was concentrated on political reform.

- The power of political parties, Progressives believed, could be diminished in two ways.
    1. By increasing the power of the people, so they could express their will directly as voters.
    2. By placing more power in the hands of nonelective, nonpartisan officials.
- Both avenues were pursued by Progressives. In the process, political parties became less important in American life and voter participation declined.
- At the same time, interest groups—trade associations, labor organizations—began to establish their influence in American politics; and powerful party machines, such as Tammany Hall, often adopted reforms to perpetuate their influence and survival.

City politics: Progressives made urban political machines and special interest groups their targets. They were responsible for the introduction of the city commission and the city manager.

- **City commission government:** First used in 1900 in Galveston, Texas.
    1. Five commissioners are elected.
    2. Each commissioner becomes the head of one department of city government, and the five meet jointly to enact legislation.
- **City manager government:** First employed in 1913 in Dayton, Ohio.
    1. A council or a commission is elected as the policy-making body.
    2. The council or commission then hires a manager, who administers the policies and appoints subordinates.

Democratization of state governments: Progressives pushed for other reforms to limit the influence of political parties in state governments.

- First proposed by Populists, the initiative and the referendum are attempts to increase the influence of the electorate.
  1. First introduced in South Dakota in 1898, the **initiative** is a method whereby voters propose laws, either for action by the legislature or for submission to a popular vote. Usually the signatures of 15 percent of the voters are required.
  2. Adopted by Oregon in 1902, the **referendum** enables any citizen who believes a law is bad to circulate a petition asking that it be submitted to a popular vote. Such a petition must be signed by 5–10 percent of the registered voters.
- First adopted by Oregon in 1908, the **recall** gives voters the right to remove a public official from office before the expiration of his/her term.
  1. Usually a new election is held when a certain portion (10–30 percent) of the voters demand it.
  2. If not reelected, the official is recalled.
- Initiated by Progressives to improve the quality of elected officials, the **direct primary** was first adopted by Mississippi in 1902. It allows voters to select the nominees for political office.

Robert M. LaFollette: Although he was a congressman (1885–91) and a U.S. senator (1906–25), he is most often remembered as governor of Wisconsin (1900–06).

- He sought to enhance the public interest and turned Wisconsin into a **"laboratory of progressivism."**
- The state served as a model for progressive reform, and as its spokesman LaFollette became a national progressive leader during the early years of this century.
- He was highly effective in publicizing progressivism nationwide.
- In 1911 he became leader of the Progressive movement and organized the **National Progressive Republican League** for the purpose of liberalizing the Republican Party.
- Republicans who were opposed to the conservatism of President **William Taft** became League supporters. Its formation split the Republican Party into liberal and conservative factions and resulted in the creation of the **Progressive Party.**

Key 23 Social and economic reform

OVERVIEW *Progressives also channeled their energies toward **moral reform** in their quest to improve human behavior by improving the social environment. These campaigns included the **temperance crusade** and efforts to **curb prostitution,** as well as reforms that involved **restricting immigration, curbing monopolies,** and attaining **suffrage for women.***

Women's Christian Temperance Union (1873): Founded by temperance advocates in Chicago and after 1879 led by **Frances Willard,** its purpose was to promote temperance through education and the enactment of legislation. It publicized the connection between alcohol and family violence, unemployment, poverty, and disease.

Anti-Saloon League: Founded in Oberlin, Ohio, in 1893, it focused attention on the saloon and opposed the sale of alcoholic beverages by carrying on vigorous lobbying for **Prohibition by Constitutional amendment.**
- Together with the Women's Christian Temperance Union, it publicized the connection between alcohol and health problems such as liver disease.
- It also attempted to link the drinking that saloons encouraged with accidents, poverty, and impaired industrial productivity.

Webb-Kenyon Act (1913): Passed over President **Taft's veto,** it prohibited the transportation of alcoholic beverages into dry states where it was intended they would be used to violate local laws.

Volstead Act (1919): Passed in 1919 over President **Wilson's veto,** it defined liquor as any beverage containing more than 0.5 percent alcohol. It went into effect on January 16, 1920 and provided the enforcement apparatus for the **Eighteenth Amendment.** It established penalties for violation of the law and created the post of commissioner of prohibition, under the Bureau of Internal Revenue, to administer the law.

Eighteenth Amendment (1920): This amendment prohibited the manufacture, sale or transportation of alcoholic beverages. It was ratified on January 29, 1919 and went into effect on January 16, 1920. It was repealed with the adoption of the Twenty-first Amendment in 1933.

Dillingham Commission: Chaired by Senator **William P. Dillingham** of Vermont, this commission of "experts" studied the problem of immigration.

- Its report concluded that the newer immigrants, those from southern and eastern Europe, were less likely to assimilate than previous immigrants.
- It implied that immigration should be restricted by nationality.
- Such recommendations were applied in 1917 when a literacy test requirement was passed, which mandated that all immigrants pass a test in English or in another language in order to enter and stay in the United States.

Mann or White Slave Traffic Act (1910): Interstate and international transportation of women for immoral purposes was prohibited.

- Congress was moved to respond when **muckraker** publicity exposed rings that kidnapped young women and forced them into prostitution.
- By 1915, almost every state had outlawed brothels and prostitution.

Suffrage movement: This movement, begun during the mid-nineteenth century, became the single largest reform movement during the Progressive Era.

- With better organization and greater political sophistication, substantial victories were won by the suffrage movement.
- Although the **National and American Women Suffrage Association (NAWSA)** had been formed in 1890, it was rejuvenated in 1915 when **Carrie Chapman Catt,** a skilled political organizer, became its president.
- Under her guidance, NAWSA pushed for a federal suffrage amendment.
- In 1920, the **Nineteenth Amendment** was finally ratified.

Alice Paul: In 1913 she established the **Congressional Union,** which pushed for a federal women's suffrage amendment.

- In 1916 the Congressional Union organized the **National Women's Party** to lend political support to government officials in favor of suffrage for women.
- The party used militant tactics of the English suffragettes that Paul had learned while in England. The tactics included hunger strikes, picketing, and sending delegations to the president.
- Following the ratification of the Nineteenth Amendment, Paul wrote the so-called **Alice Paul Amendment,** a version of the **Equal Rights Amendment,** which was introduced at the National Women's Party convention in 1923.

Key 24 Roosevelt's Square Deal administration

OVERVIEW *Progressivism made its debut on the national level with Theodore Roosevelt, who introduced a new activist role for the chief executive.*

Vice president and president: When **William McKinley** was assassinated, Vice President **Theodore Roosevelt** became president on September 14, 1901.
- Grew politically powerful, gained control of the Republican Party, and demonstrated legislative leadership in advocating Progressive reforms.
- Inaugurated federal regulation of economic affairs.

Northern Securities **v.** *United States* **(1902):** One of the highly publicized cases, initiated by Roosevelt, that sought to regulate trusts, with the government serving as mediator.
- He ordered the Justice Department to use the **Sherman Antitrust Act** against this railroad monopoly in the Northwest.
- By 1904, the Supreme Court had ruled that the Northern Securities Company be dissolved.
- This case aided in identifying Roosevelt as a **"trust buster,"** although more prosecutions of trusts took place during **Taft's** administration.

Department of Commerce and Labor (1903): Created to regulate business and enforce economic regulations.
- Some agencies in the department included: the Census Bureau, Patent Office, Coast and Geodetic Survey, Bureau of Standards, Inland Waterways Authority, Weather Bureau, Bureau of Labor Statistics, Bureau of Labor Standards, Women's Division, Wages and Hours and Public Contracts Division, and Bureau of Corporations.
- In 1913, the two departments were separated.

Bureau of Corporations (1903): Was empowered to investigate interstate corporations and to report on their activities. In 1914, the **Federal Trade Commission** replaced it.

Elkins Act (1903): Amended the **Interstate Commerce Act** of 1887 by forbidding rebates, defining unfair discrimination, and reinforcing adherence to published rates by interstate shippers.

Election of 1904: Theodore Roosevelt defeated the Democratic candidate, **Alton B. Parker,** a judge in the New York Supreme Court from 1885 to 1904.

- Roosevelt received over 57 percent of the popular vote and promised to bring a **"square deal"** to every citizen.
- The term meant that he would use the presidency to ensure the safety, happiness, and prosperity of the public by solving social problems, promoting conservation, regulating big business, and controlling the railroads.

Lockner **v.** *New York* **(1905):** The U.S. Supreme Court ruled that a New York law limiting working hours was unconstitutional. It was judged to be an infringement upon the contract rights between the employer and his/her employees.

- The decision was modified in *Muller* **v.** *Oregon* **(1908),** when the U.S. Supreme Court upheld an Oregon statute that limited the length of the workday for women to 10 hours.

Hepburn Act (1906): Amended the **Interstate Commerce Act** by enlarging the commission to seven members and by giving it authority to determine railroad rates and to prescribe bookkeeping methods for companies. It also prohibited free passes and forbade railroad companies to carry goods produced by themselves.

Upton Sinclair: An author whose muckraking disclosures in *The Jungle* regarding meat packing and later articles on patent medicine prompted federal legislation.

- The **Meat Inspection Act (1906)** authorized the Secretary of Agriculture to undertake the inspection of all meat products shipped in interstate commerce to make certain they were fit for human consumption and were packed under sanitary conditions.
- The **Pure Food and Drug Act (1906)** forbade the manufacture, sale, or transportation of adulterated foods and drugs and the mislabeling of such products involved in interstate commerce.

Panic of 1907: A short, sharp depression, largely caused by the failure of the **Knickerbocker Trust Company** in New York, which weakened confidence in banks.

- The stock market decline caused many banks to close and led to a money shortage.
- Financial titan **J. P. Morgan** helped construct a pool of the assets of several key New York banks to prop up shaky financial institutions.
- By 1908, recovery had begun.

Aldrich-Vreeland Act (1908): Provided for a more flexible currency.

- Permitted banks to issue circulating notes based on commercial paper and on state and municipal bonds.
- Created the **National Monetary Commission** to study the entire question of banking and currency.

KEY FIGURE

Theodore Roosevelt: State legislator (1882–84), police commissioner of New York City (1895–97), Rough Rider colonel in the Spanish-American War after resigning as assistant secretary of the navy (1897–98), governor of New York (1899–1900), and finally vice president, he became a leading Progressive president of the United States.

Key 25 Roosevelt's conservation policies

OVERVIEW *Theodore Roosevelt initiated a policy that attempted to curb the destruction of the wilderness at a time when only 10 percent of the forests remained from the initial period of colonization in America.*

Forest Reserve Act (1891): Authorized the president to set aside forest areas in any part of the national domain and establish them as national parks. Under this act, Roosevelt set aside 150,000,000 acres, much more than his three predecessors.

Newlands Reclamation Act (1902): Provided that income from the sale of public land in 16 western states be used for building and maintaining irrigation projects in arid regions. Reclaimed land would then be sold to settlers at low prices.

Inland Waterways Commission (1907): Created by President Roosevelt, the commission made a survey of the relation of river, soil, and forests to water power development and water transportation.

White House Conservation Conference: Called by President Roosevelt in 1908, attendees included congressmen, his cabinet, the Supreme Court, and governors of 34 states.
- It emphasized and publicized the issue of conservation.
- Made recommendations for the conservation and improvement of all the natural resources of the nation.

National Conservation Commission: Established in 1908 by President Roosevelt, the commission, chaired by **Gifford Pinchot,** attempted to inventory America's natural resources and then recommended that 234 million acres of land be set aside for public use.

KEY FIGURE

Gifford Pinchot: The first professional forester in the United States and chief of the U.S. Forestry Service (1898–1910), he advocated rational and efficient use of the wilderness.

Key 26 Taft as successor

OVERVIEW *When Theodore Roosevelt followed through on his promise not to seek reelection in 1908, he supported his secretary of war, William Howard Taft, for president. The direction in which Roosevelt had moved the government changed when the "old guard" gained a foothold during the Taft administration.*

William Howard Taft: As the Republican candidate, Taft defeated Democrat **William Jennings Bryan** and Socialist **Eugene V. Debs.**
- Before serving in Roosevelt's cabinet (1904–08), Taft had been the first civil governor of the Philippines (1901–04).
- Although he had compiled a stronger record on protecting the wilderness and had prosecuted more trusts than Roosevelt, he ended up the captive of conservatives.
- He backed the income tax and direct election of senators, but lacked Roosevelt's ability to maneuver and to publicize the issues he supported.

Payne-Aldrich Tariff (1909): Basically protectionist, the tariff favored Eastern industry.
- For example, duties on cotton and wool goods were increased.
- This measure was not considered a tariff reform as promised by Taft and the Republicans. The overall average of the tariff was about 37 percent.

Joseph Cannon: A powerful and conservative speaker of the U.S. House of Representatives while Taft was president, "Uncle Joe" Cannon controlled the Rules Committee and became a virtual dictator over the legislative process in Congress.
- In 1910, a coalition of **insurgents** (Republicans) and Democrats led a revolt that expanded the membership of the Rules Committee from 5 to 15, had members elected rather than appointed, and specifically barred the speaker of the House from membership on the committee.
- Cannon was defeated for reelection in 1912, although Taft had supported him in order to secure his backing for legislation that the administration favored.

Pinchot-Ballinger affair: Chief of the U.S. Forestry Service **Gifford Pinchot** accused Secretary of the Interior **Richard A. Ballinger** of allowing private interests to exploit coal mining and timber areas of the United States for his personal profit, thereby betraying conservation policy.

- Ballinger had removed 1 million acres of forest and mineral land from the reserved list.
- After asking the U.S. attorney general to investigate, Taft announced his support for Ballinger.
- When Pinchot asked Congress to investigate the matter, Taft dismissed him.
- The congressional committee also exonerated Ballinger.
- This episode contributed to splitting the Republican Party.

Mann-Elkins Act (1910): Designed to strengthen the power of the **Interstate Commerce Commission (ICC),** the act authorized it to regulate the communications industry.

- Telegraph, telephone, and cable corporations were put under ICC jurisdiction.
- The commission was given authority to suspend rate increases until they were determined to be reasonable.

Postal Savings Bank System (1910): The Post Office Department was authorized to receive savings deposits from individuals and to pay interest of 2 percent per year on such deposits.

***United States* v. *American Tobacco Company* (1911):** The government prosecuted the American Tobacco Company for violating antitrust laws.

- The U.S. Supreme Court ordered the company to reorganize on the basis of the "rule of reason" but did not order its dissolution.
- This meant that only reasonable restraints of trade were authorized.

***Standard Oil Company* v. *United States* (1911):** A government suit by the Taft administration charged that the Standard Oil Company had violated the antimonopoly clause of the Sherman Act by acquiring the Tennessee Coal and Iron Company in 1907.

- The suit became an affair of personal honor and a question of broad principle to Roosevelt.
- He had approved the acquisition because United States Steel representatives had deemed it necessary to prevent a financial collapse on Wall Street.

Progressive or Bull Moose Party (1912): The Progressive element in the Republican Party led by **Robert M. LaFollette** opposed Taft's conservative policies.

- Refusing to support Taft's nomination in 1912, this element formed the **Progressive Party.**

- When it became clear that Taft controlled the Republican convention, the Progressives named Theodore Roosevelt as their candidate for president.
  1. Roosevelt espoused the **New Nationalism** as his platform, which included support for a federal child labor law, federal workman's compensation, regulation of labor relations, and a minimum wage for women.
  2. Also advocated were tariff reform, women's suffrage, the initiative, referendum, and recall, direct election of senators, direct primaries, and antitrust legislation.

Election of 1912: Woodrow Wilson, the Democrat, was the victor over **William Howard Taft,** the Republican; **Theodore Roosevelt,** the Progressive; and **Eugene V. Debs,** the Socialist. The split in the Republican Party, after which the Progressive Party was formed, contributed to the Democratic victory.

Key 27 Wilson's New Freedom administration

OVERVIEW *Born in Virginia and raised in South Carolina, Woodrow Wilson was president of Princeton University and governor of New Jersey before serving two terms as president of the United States (1913–21). While initially differing from Theodore Roosevelt on the direction of Progressive philosophy, he later advocated many of his ideas.*

Woodrow Wilson: He advocated a different brand of progressivism, described by supporters as the **"New Freedom."**
- Unlike Theodore Roosevelt, Wilson advocated the elimination of monopolies. To him, bigness in business was unjust and inefficient.
- As a supporter of Progressive legislation, he advocated tariff reform, income tax reform, currency and credit reform, and antitrust legislation.
- Eventually he capitulated to the programs of the New Nationalism by sponsoring measures that expanded the role of the national government in regulating the economy and in shaping the economic and social structure as well.

Underwood-Simmons Tariff (1913): Reduced tariff rates on many items and placed others (e.g., wool, hides, iron ore, steel rails) on the free list.
- The average tariff rate was lowered to about 27 percent.
- The act also imposed a tax, made constitutional by the Sixteenth Amendment, on incomes of $4,000 and over, with graduated tax rates rising to 6 percent on incomes over $500,000.

Federal Reserve Act (1913): Also known as the **Glass-Owen Act,** it provided a flexible currency system that could adjust to the needs of the economy and reform what President Wilson referred to as the money monopoly.
- The act created a **Federal Reserve system** of 12 districts with a **Federal Reserve bank** in each district.
- These banks were depositories for the cash reserves of all national banks and of other banks and trust companies joining the system.
- These banks would use these reserves to support loans to private

banks at an interest or "discount" rate set by the Federal Reserve system.

- Federal Reserve notes, a new type of paper currency, would be issued by regional Federal Reserve banks. Such currency would become the nation's basic medium of trade and was also backed by the government.
- Funds could be shifted when necessary to troubled areas to meet credit demands or to protect banks.
- A Federal Reserve Board of seven members (later eight) appointed by the president was established to supervise the activities of the Federal Reserve system.

Federal Trade Commission Act (1914): Created a five-member Federal Trade Commission authorized to investigate the operations of corporations, to require them to publish reports on their activities, and to issue cease-and-desist orders against any corporation found guilty of practicing unfair methods of competition, which were not specifically defined.

Clayton Antitrust Act (1914): Designed to strengthen the **Sherman Antitrust Act** of 1890 by declaring illegal certain corporate practices not included in the Sherman Act.

- The definition of "unfair methods of competition" was expanded to include price discrimination, interlocking directorates, purchase by one company of stock in competing corporations, and contracts limiting the right of purchasers to handle the products of competing companies.
- Officers of corporations were made liable for illegal acts of the corporation.
- The use of injunctions in labor disputes was prohibited unless necessary to prevent damage to property.
- Labor unions and agricultural associations were exempted from antitrust acts, and strikes, boycotts, and peaceful picketing were deemed legal processes.

Keating-Owen Act (1916): Invalidated in 1918 by the Supreme Court, this act, which Wilson supported, forbade shipment in interstate commerce of products made by companies employing children under 14 and by mines employing children under 16.

Federal Farm Loan Act (1916): Created a **Federal Farm Loan Board** and 12 regional Farm Loan banks authorized to make loans to cooperative Farm Loan Associations, which in turn made loans to individual farmers at low interest rates.

Smith-Hughes Act (1917): Made government-sponsored courses in vocational agriculture and other subjects available in high schools.
- Created a **Federal Board for Vocational Education.**
- Made funding available for training in agriculture and other vocational areas.

Louis Brandeis: An outstanding Harvard Law School graduate, he became a major figure in the Progressive movement because of his investigations of monopoly power.
- Woodrow Wilson nominated him to the Supreme Court in 1916 and after 5 months of bitter controversy in the Senate, he was confirmed.
- As the first Jew to serve on the Court, he was a supporter of social reform.
- Known for the "Brandeis brief," his scholarly approach to written decisions is still admired today.

Amendments: Four changes to the Constitution made during the two Wilson administrations reflected, in part, the progressive mood of the nation.
- **Sixteenth Amendment (1913):** Congress may tax incomes.
- **Seventeenth Amendment (1913):** Senators are to be elected directly by the people.
- **Eighteenth Amendment (1919):** National prohibition of the making and distributing of alcoholic beverages is imposed.
- **Nineteenth Amendment (1920):** Women gain the right to vote.

Theme 6 AMERICAN IMPERIALISM

*D*uring the 1890s, the United States began to acquire territories beyond its continental borders. This era of colonial expansion was replicated by other leading Western industrial nations. From these imperialistic ventures grew premises that would shape American foreign policy in the future. Problems also emerged out of America's imperial experience.

Key 28 Imperialism: Reasons and theories

OVERVIEW *Many reasons account for what is sometimes called the* **New Manifest Destiny,** *a time when American foreign policy was affected by economic, social, and political conditions at home and the increasing need, as some saw it, to participate in expansion beyond the continental United States.*

Background: Several theories suggest the purposes behind U.S. imperialism.
- America's treatment of Native Americans had established a precedent for exerting colonial control over dependent peoples.
- Popularized by historian Frederick Jackson Turner, the idea that America's frontier had closed produced fears regarding the nation's future supply of natural resources. Why not acquire new sources abroad?
- The **depression of 1893** persuaded some businessmen that new overseas markets should be sought for U.S. products.
- Some politicians favored an **aggressive foreign policy** to focus attention away from the decade's current problems and protests.
- The **competitive spirit** played a role since Americans did not want to be excluded from the imperialist drive among Europeans.
- **Improvements in transportation and communication** also increased America's involvement in world affairs.
- **Technological improvements** in industry increased output and indicated the need for additional foreign markets.
- Philosophical reasons were also offered for expansion.

Imperialist argument: A distortion of Charles Darwin's theories formed a basis for rationalizing expansionism. According to this argument, since nations or "races," like biological species, struggled for existence, and only the fittest could survive, it followed that strong nations would inevitably dominate weak ones in accordance with the law of nature.

Josiah Strong: A Congregational clergyman and advocate of overseas missionary work, Strong advanced the imperialist argument in *Our Country: Its Possible Future and Its Present Crisis.*

- This publication proclaimed that the Anglo-Saxon "race" was "divinely commissioned" to spread its institutions throughout the world.
- Americans, as adherents of civil liberty and Christianity, were members of a God-favored race destined to lead the world.

Alfred T. Mahan: A captain and later an admiral in the navy, Mahan was one of the most capable and effective advocates of imperialism, who expressed his philosophy in *The Influence of Sea Power upon History, 1660–1783* (1890), *The Influence of Sea Power upon the French Revolution and Empire, 1793–1812* (1892), and *The Interest of America in Sea Power* (1897).

- He argued that industrialization required markets, some overseas.
- A merchant marine and a navy, combined with coal stations and repair yards, were required to reach such markets. These stations meant colonies.
- A colonial empire would result in the growth of national wealth and power.
- Mahan's ideas so influenced policymakers that by 1900 the U.S. Navy was the third most powerful fleet in the world.

KEY QUOTATION

Whether they will or not, Americans must now begin to look outward.

Alfred Thayer Mahan

Key 29 Political developments
enhancing expansionism

OVERVIEW *Stirrings of imperialism became manifest in America's attitude and approach to foreign policy at the close of the nineteenth century.*

Hemispheric hegemony: Foreign policy now emphasized U.S. influence in the Western Hemisphere.
* Both James G. Blaine and Richard Oleny, as secretaries of state, exhibited a new, assertive diplomacy.
* Their policies helped to pave the way for the Spanish-American War.

Pan American Conference (1889): At the initiative of **Benjamin Harrison's** secretary of state, **James G. Blaine,** the first Pan-American Congress took place in October of 1889.
* Delegates from 19 American nations were present.
* Blaine's proposals—the creation of an inter-American customs union, and arbitration procedures to resolve disputes—were rejected, but an **International Bureau of American Republics** was established.

Richard Olney: As Cleveland's secretary of state, Richard Olney had an aggressive approach to foreign policy, which nearly led to war in 1895.
* A long-standing boundary dispute between Venezuela and British Guiana assumed grave importance when gold was found in the disputed territory.
* The United States demanded that Great Britain accept arbitration and Olney asserted that Great Britain was violating the Monroe Doctrine.
* At first Britain rejected arbitration, but agreed to it after military force was threatened.
* In 1897, the British signed a treaty with Venezuela, providing for an arbitration commission.

Hawaii: Serving as a stopover station for American ships and a destination for missionaries, Hawaii assumed greater political and economic importance during the second half of the nineteenth century.

- An 1875 treaty with Hawaii allowed Hawaiian sugar to enter the United States duty-free but directed Hawaii not to make territorial or economic concessions to other nations.
- A new treaty signed in 1887 renewed the existing agreement and provided for the leasing of Pearl Harbor as a naval station.
- When Hawaii's **Queen Liliuokalani** tried to eliminate American influence there, U.S. settlers overthrew her and set up a government establishing the Republic of Hawaii.
- This provisional government sought annexation as early as 1893.
- After much debate, Hawaii was finally annexed in 1898.

Samoa: In 1878, a native prince from Samoa signed a treaty providing for an American naval station at Pago Pago, as well as for U.S. military aid in negotiating any differences between a foreign power and Samoa.
- Thereafter, Great Britain and Germany also secured treaty rights, and in 1889 war seemed imminent among the three powers.
- After a tropical hurricane dispersed their ships, Germany, Great Britain, and the United States established a tripartite protectorate over Samoa.
- By 1899, the United States and Germany had divided the islands between them, while Britain received other Pacific territories as compensation.

Key 30 Spanish-American War

OVERVIEW *Although U.S. imperial ambitions existed well before 1900, the war with Spain in 1898 exemplified America's expansionism most graphically. It left the nation with an overseas empire and made the United States a leading world power. With victory also came the problem of leading and running an empire.*

First stages of the Spanish-American War: The United States declared war against Spain on April 25, 1898. Causes included:
- The American tariff policy with its high duties, which hurt the Cuban economy.
- U.S. protests against Spanish treatment of Cuban natives.
- The threat to American investments in Cuba.
- **The deLome Letter (1898):** Written by Duprey deLome, Spanish minister to the United States, to a friend in Cuba, it described President **William McKinley** as a weak man and "a bidder for the admiration of the crowd."
  1. Stolen by a Cuban agent from the Havana mail, the letter appeared in many newspapers across America.
  2. deLome resigned immediately.
  3. Many believed that the letter was intentionally leaked to the press.
- **The sinking of the U.S. battleship** *Maine:* One of the key events that precipitated the Spanish-American War, this occurred in Havana harbor on February 15, 1898, as the result of an explosion. (Later an investigation suggested that the explosion was accidental.)
  1. The death of 266 American sailors was attributed to the Spanish, and **"Remember the Maine!"** became a national chant for revenge.
  2. Congress appropriated $50 million for military preparations for war.

Teller amendment: A statement approved by Congress, it disclaimed any intention on the part of the United States to extend "sovereignty, jurisdiction, or control" over Cuba except for the purpose of pacification, and was designed as an assurance that U.S. efforts to assist Cuba were not motivated by a desire to annex it.

Rough Riders: This volunteer cavalry regiment organized by **Theodore Roosevelt** consisted of men from as diverse backgrounds as the Western frontier and colleges in the East.

- They were best known for their charge up **San Juan Hill** (actually Kettle Hill) in Cuba on July 1, 1898, in which a heavily fortified position was seized.
- Their exploits helped launch Theodore Roosevelt as a war hero.
- This regiment was typical of the community-based, amateur military units that did the bulk of the fighting during the war.

Commodore George Dewey: Instructed by President McKinley's assistant secretary of the navy, Theodore Roosevelt, to attack the Philippines in the event of war, Dewey left China and headed for Manila after the start of the Spanish-American War.
- He became the first hero of the war (and was immediately promoted to admiral) after the 7-hour **Battle of Manila Bay.**
- The Spanish fleet was destroyed, but the Spaniards continued to hold Manila until an American expeditionary force took the city on August 13, 1898.

Battle of Santiago: In July 1898 a Spanish fleet under Admiral **Pascual Cervera,** which had been in Santiago harbor (Cuba), was blockaded by the U.S. fleet under Admiral **William T. Sampson.**
- In the battle, the Spanish fleet was destroyed.
- When the U.S. Army attacked the city from the rear, Cervera fled.

Treaty of Paris: Signed on December 10, 1898, in Paris, it ended the Spanish-American War, which had resulted in the loss of 5,000 lives (only 379 were battle casualties) and had cost about $250 million.
- Under its terms, Spain was to withdraw from Cuba and to recognize its independence.
- The United States received Puerto Rico, Guam, and the Philippines, while Spain received $420 million from the United States.

Anti-imperialist League (1898): This organization was established by upper-class Bostonians, New Yorkers, and others to fight annexation, particularly of the Philippines.
- Attracted many supporters in the Northeast and vigorously campaigned against the Treaty of Paris.
- Was unable to prevent ratification of the treaty.

Armed forces overhauled: The war experience led to a major overhaul of the armed forces under Secretary of War **Elihu Root's** supervision.
- Central to his reforms was the establishment, in 1903, of a **general staff** to act as military adviser to the secretary of war.
- The general staff, a central planning agency modeled on similar bodies in Europe, aimed to supervise and coordinate the army establishment.

Key 31   Foreign policy in Latin America under Theodore Roosevelt

OVERVIEW *In its effort to achieve hemispheric hege-mony, the United States moved toward a restatement of the Monroe Doctrine.*

Canal Zone: Actions and events included:
- **Hay-Pauncefote Treaty (1901):** This agreement with Great Britain gave the United States the right to construct and control a canal across Central America that would be open to all nations in time of war and peace. The United States agreed to maintain the neutrality of the canal.
- **Spooner Act (1902):** This act authorized the purchase of the French rights for construction of a canal in Panama for $40 million, and the negotiation of an agreement with Colombia to grant control of the region for the United States. If Colombia refused, the president could then make a similar treaty with Nicaragua.
- **Hay-Herran Treaty (1903):** Although it was never approved by the Colombian Senate, this agreement with the Republic of Colombia would have given the United States a 99-year lease on a canal zone 6 miles wide in the Colombia province of Panama in return for an initial payment of $10 million and $250,000 yearly thereafter.
- **Panama Revolution (1903):** When the Hay-Herran Treaty was not approved, Panamanian rebels revolted and proclaimed Panama a republic. Immediately thereafter, the United States recognized Panama's independence.
- **Hay-Bunau Varilla Treaty (1903):** This agreement between the United States and Panama leased the Canal Zone, which was 10 miles wide, to the United States in perpetuity for an initial payment of $10 million and $250,000 yearly beginning 9 years after approval of the treaty. The Panama Canal opened in 1914.

Cuba: The **Platt Amendment,** passed by Congress in 1901, left Cuba only nominally independent.
- According to its provisions, Cuba was to make no treaties that would impair its independence or to assume debts that it could not pay.
- The naval base at **Guantanamo** was to be leased to the United States.

- To preserve Cuba's independence, America could intervene in Cuba when necessary.
- These provisions were incorporated into Cuba's constitution.

Puerto Rico: Legislation included:
- **Foraker Act (1900):** This congressional act created a civil government for the territory of Puerto Rico.
  1. It provided for an elected assembly and an executive council of 11 members, appointed by the President of the United States to serve as an upper house.
- The U.S. President would also appoint a president-general.
- **Jones Act (1917):** This act made Puerto Rico an unincorporated territory.
  1. Puerto Ricans were granted U.S. citizenship and home rule through an elected legislature.
  2. The president of the United States appointed the governor and supreme court.

Roosevelt Corollary (1904): This message to Congress exemplified Roosevelt's belief that the United States should assume international police power in the Western Hemisphere and prevent European interference, thereby justifying intervention in Latin American affairs.
- This philosophy grew out of Roosevelt's interpretation of the **Monroe Doctrine.**
- The paternal and dominating role of the United States is illustrated in the **Venezuela debt dispute** (1902) and the **Dominican debt default** (1904–05).
- Between 1900 and 1917, American troops intervened in Cuba, Panama, the Dominican Republic, Mexico, Nicaragua, and Haiti.

KEY QUOTATION

Walk softly, but carry a big stick.

President Theodore Roosevelt
in a message to Congress, 1904

Key 32 Latin American policy under Taft and Wilson

OVERVIEW *The years after Theodore Roosevelt's presidency have been labeled as reflecting "dollar diplomacy" in American foreign policy. Under President Taft, American investments in the Caribbean grew dramatically, and military intervention was used in Honduras, Haiti, Nicaragua, Mexico, and the Dominican Republic to protect those investments. Woodrow Wilson continued this policy of intervention.*

Dollar diplomacy: Philander C. Knox, Taft's secretary of state, was responsible for the "dollar diplomacy" that promoted business interests overseas.
- Diplomatic and military protection was provided for such enterprises.
- This policy lasted until the 1930s.

Woodrow Wilson: As president, Wilson exhibited both remarkable vision in foreign policy and an inflexible, self-righteous morality. American intervention continued in the Caribbean and in Latin America.

Dominican Republic: The United States established a military government there in 1916 after marines landed in Haiti to quell a revolution. United States forces remained until 1934.

Relations with Mexico: Wilson's four-year policy left a lasting hostility toward the United States.
- **General Victoriano Huerta:** Reactionary president of Mexico, in 1913 he had deposed Francisco Madero, whom Huerta's government murdered.
  1. That same year, Huerta established a military dictatorship.
  2. In 1914 a minor naval incident provided the United States with an opportunity to occupy the Mexican port of Veracruz.

ABC Conference: Held in 1914 in Niagara Falls, Ontario, this conference proposed that the Huerta government be eliminated and a provisional government be established.
  1. It was designed to iron out differences between rival factions of Huerta and Venustiano Carranza in Mexico.

2. The United States, Argentina, Brazil, and Chile sent representatives.

- **Venustiano Carranza:** His election under a new constitution, adopted in early 1917, led to formal recognition of the Mexican government by the United States, with preliminary recognition coming as early as 1915.
- **Francisco (Pancho) Villa:** Carranza's erstwhile lieutenant, a Mexican revolutionary leader and outlaw, he made several raids into the United States.
  1. In January 1916 a raid in New Mexico left 17 Americans dead.
  2. With the permission of the Carranza government, President Wilson sent General **John J. Pershing** into Mexico with an expeditionary force to capture Villa.
  3. The attempt proved fruitless.

Key 33 Foreign policy in Asia

OVERVIEW *America's colonial empire included Puerto Rico, Alaska, Hawaii, part of Samoa, Guam, the Philippines, and a chain of minor Pacific islands. The United States soon discovered that, to preserve and maintain its overseas empire, it had to stockpile armaments, modify its policy of refraining from alliances, and deal with Far Eastern international politics.*

Insular cases: Supreme Court cases (e.g., *DeLima* v. *Bidwell, Downes* v. *Bidwell*), sought to define the status of alien peoples in the newly acquired territories with respect to the rights of American citizens.
- Court distinguished between **"incorporated"** and **"unincorporated"** territories.
- The Court held that constitutional rights and privileges did not automatically apply to these areas, the insular territories, but Congress could grant such rights and privileges as it desired.

Philippine insurrection: After the Spanish-American War, **Emilio Aguinaldo** led an uprising of Filipinos against U.S. control of their homeland.
- The armed revolt began on February 4, 1899, and continued into 1902.
- Aguinaldo was captured by U.S. forces in 1901, and then declared his allegiance to America.

Schurman Commission (1899): Led by **Jacob G. Schurman,** this five-man commission investigated conditions in the Philippines to determine how to set up a civil government. It recommended U.S. rule until the Philippines were prepared for self-government.

Philippine commission (1900): Headed by **William Howard Taft,** appointed civil governor of the Philippines in 1901, the commission had as its purpose the reconstruction of the civil government of the Philippines.

Philippine Government Act (1902): Made the Philippines an unincorporated U.S. Territory.
- Philippine residents were granted citizenship.
- The **Taft Commission** was to remain as the governing body until a two-house legislature was established, with the lower house to be an elected body.

Jones Act (1916): Promised independence for the Philippines when a stable government had been established.
- Granted Filipino citizenship to the inhabitants.
- Provided for a government that would consist of an elected legislature and a governor-general to be appointed by the president of the United States.

Treaty of Portsmouth (1905): Signed in New Hampshire, this agreement ended the **Russo-Japanese War** (1904–05).
- President **Theodore Roosevelt** acted as a mediator in ending this conflict by inviting representatives of both powers to negotiate a settlement.
- Both nations agreed to recognize the neutrality of all Chinese territory outside of Manchuria.
- Roosevelt received a Nobel Prize for his intervention.

Taft-Katsura Agreement (1905): Under its terms, the United States promised not to interfere with Japan's ambitions in Korea in exchange for Japan's pledge to respect U.S. control of the Philippines. The purpose was to provide some assurance that Japan's control in the Far East would be limited.

Root-Takahira Agreement (1908): Under this executive agreement with Japan, the two countries agreed to maintain the status quo in the Pacific, to respect each other's territories in the Pacific, and to support the **"open door policy"** in China and China's independence and territorial integrity.

Boxer Rebellion (1900): An uprising instigated by a secret Chinese society known as the Boxers, it was designed to drive foreigners out of China.
- About 300 people were killed, and the British embassy in Peking was attacked.
- European, U.S., and Japanese troops suppressed the rebellion.
- Foreign powers received compensation from the Chinese.

KEY FIGURE

John Hay: President McKinley's secretary of state, he initiated the "open door policy" with China by sending notes to Germany, England, Russia, and later France, Japan, and Italy, requesting that nations holding "spheres of influence" uphold Chinese customs and preserve Chinese independence and territorial integrity.

Theme 7 WORLD WAR I

*K*nown at the time as the Great War, World War I was the first truly "total" war. Americans became involved in it 3 years after it had begun. Although the war was devastating to Western Europe, the United States suffered much lower casualties. As one of the victors in the war, the United States was launched into a position of international leadership.

Before long the nation became frustrated and disillusioned, realizing that the world had not been made "safe for democracy" as President Wilson had promised. Economically, however, the war sparked an industrial boom that launched the prosperous 1920s. On the negative side, the war awakened intolerance, hatred, and bigotry in its quest for social unity on the homefront. It also assisted in the demise of progressivism.

INDIVIDUAL KEYS IN THIS THEME

Key 34 Prelude to American involvement

OVERVIEW *For 3 years, the United States attempted to maintain neutrality and stay out of the war, but this goal proved to be virtually impossible.*

Initial events: World War I began on June 28, 1914, when Archduke Franz Ferdinand, heir to the Austro-Hungarian Empire, was assassinated by a Serbian nationalist while visiting Sarajevo, a provincial capital in the Austro-Hungarian Empire, which Slavic nationalists wanted to annex and make part of Serbia.
  • By August 6, 1914, Germany, France, Great Britain, Russia, and the Austro-Hungarian Empire had all declared war.
  • Italy, the Ottoman Empire, and other nations joined the war later in 1914.

Triple Alliance: The alliance, composed of Germany, Italy, and Austria-Hungary, also called the **Central Powers,** formed one of the two opposing camps in Western Europe on the eve of World War I.

Triple Entente: This entente, consisting of France, Great Britain, and Russia, known as the **Allies,** was organized to create a "balance of power" in Western Europe against the nations of the Triple Alliance.

Orders in Council: Issued by Great Britain at the start of World War I, the orders established an Allied blockade around Germany, extended the list of contraband items, and declared the North Sea and English channel "military areas." The orders led the Germans to start a policy of unrestricted **submarine warfare** to eliminate the blockade.

American neutrality: Although President Wilson urged America to be "impartial in thought as well as deed" and issued a proclamation of neutrality on August 4, 1914, he was an admirer of Great Britain's traditions, culture, and political system.
  • He and other Americans imbued a moral quality to the Allied position, and British reports of German atrocities added to American support of the Allied cause.
  • Because war orders from France and Britain were so economically lucrative for the United States, Wilson realized by 1915 that this country could no longer remain neutral. He believed America must become the arsenal of the Allies.

- The American response to German violations of neutral rights became harsh and uncompromising.

Lusitania (1915): The *Lusitania,* a British passenger liner, was sunk by a German U-boat. When Wilson learned that 128 Americans had died, he demanded that Germany respect the rights of neutral nations, which included the American right to travel on nonmilitary vessels of warring nations.

Preparedness movement: This movement advocated building up our national defenses and preparing for involvement in the war. By the end of 1915, President Wilson had advocated a preparedness program to Congress, and rearmament was under way by the summer of 1916.

Sussex pledge (1916): An unarmed French steamer, the *Sussex,* was attacked by Germany and several American passengers were injured.
- Because of Wilson's protests, Germany pledged not to sink passenger vessels without warning and agreed to safeguard noncombatants.
- Nevertheless, torpedo attacks began again in January 1917.

Council of National Defense (1916): Created by Congress, it coordinated industry and the nation's resources for the support of national security.
- The council consisted of six cabinet members and an advisory board of seven experts from labor and industry.
- Connected to it was a **Civilian Advisory Commission,** which set up local defense councils in every state, county, and school district.

National Defense Act (1916): Provided for increasing the regular army to 175,000 and the National Guard to 450,000, and authorized the creation of military training at universities and colleges.

Merchant Marine Act (1916): Created the U.S. Shipping Board, which formed the Emergency Fleet Corporation to build, requisition, purchase, and operate merchant vessels.

Election of 1916: As the Democratic incumbent, **Woodrow Wilson** ran on the slogan "He kept us out of war."
- Promising to continue Progressive policies and to maintain peace, he won reelection, although by a small margin.
- His Republican opponent, **Charles Evans Hughes,** was an associate justice of the Supreme Court (1910–16) and later became chief justice (1930–41) during the Great Depression.

Zimmerman note: This dispatch was sent in January 1917, by Alfred Zimmerman, German Foreign Secretary, to the German representative in Mexico.
- It urged Mexico to support Germany if the United States declared war on Germany.
- In return, Mexico would receive Texas, Arizona, and New Mexico.
- The coded note was intercepted by the British, decoded, and published in the United States.
- Along with Germany's announcement on February 1, 1917, that it would sink all ships, enemy and neutral alike, the note sparked U.S. entry into the war on April 6, 1917.

Jeanette Rankin: A former suffrage organizer, in 1916 she became the first woman ever elected to Congress, where she represented Montana.
- When Congress voted on U.S. entrance into World War I, she voted no.
- In addition to being a peace activist, she supported protective legislation and Prohibition.
- In 1940 she again won election to Congress from Montana and in 1941 cast the only vote against U.S. entry into World War II.

American Expeditionary Force: Under General **John J. Pershing,** it arrived in Europe at the end of 1917.
- Assisted the Allies in halting the German advance at Chateau-Thierry, at Rheims, and later in the Argonne Forest.
- Fought for 8 months until the armistice of November 11, 1918.

Key 35   The war's effect on the
home front

OVERVIEW *At home, the nation's economic resources were mobilized, with the federal government becoming increasingly intrusive. The war accentuated social divisiveness as the federal government trampled on civil liberties.*

Selective Service Act (1917): This legislation required all males between 21 and 30 to register for military service.
- A 488,000-member army, 470,000 for the National Guard, and the conscription of 500,000 men were authorized.
- Women served in the Army and Navy Nurses Corps and in the auxiliary forces of the regular navy.

Financing the war: The war was partly financed through the sale of so-called **Liberty Bonds** to the public.
- Other revenue was raised by income taxes, excess profits taxes, inheritance taxes, and special taxes on liquor, tobacco, and theater tickets.
- The **War Revenue Act (1917)** established a graduated income tax, an excess profits tax, and an increase in excise taxes.

Committee on Public Information (CPI): Created by Congress in April 1917, the committee had as its chairman journalist **George Creel.**
- Mobilized public support of the war by explaining, through the use of pamphlets, posters, motion pictures, news stories, advertisements in magazines, pictures, and speakers, the reasons for American participation.
- Through its Division of Industrial Relations, encouraged labor to support the war.

War Industries Board (July 1917): Under financier **Bernard Baruch,** this agency organized the nation's economy.
- It regulated all war industry activities, developed new industries and sources of supply, controlled prices, and distributed and sold all war materials.
- Manufacturers who cooperated with the board's goals were exempt from antitrust laws.

Production and transportation of supplies: New agencies were set up.
- Headed by Secretary of the Treasury **William McAdoo,** the **Railroad War Board** facilitated the transportation of troops and war supplies by rail.

- Likewise, a new **Fuel Administration** was created to allocate scarce supplies of coal.
- Under the **Lever Food and Fuel Control Act,** President Wilson had authority over the production, disposition, and prices of food, fuel, and other supplies needed by the army; control extended to producers, processors, and dealers in these products.

Food Administration: Probably the most effective war agency, it supervised the feeding of the nation, its armies, and the Allies.
- **Herbert Hoover,** an engineer and business executive who later became U.S. president, was its administrator.
- He raised the price of wheat to increase production, along with encouraging voluntary conservation.
- At his suggestion, people planted "victory gardens."

Espionage Act (June 1917): A $10,000 fine and 20 years' imprisonment was prescribed for interfering with the draft or for attempting to encourage disloyalty.
- Penalties were also imposed for refusing military duty, resisting laws, or advocating treason.
- The postmaster general could ban from the mails any material he judged treasonous or seditious.

National Security League: One of several citizens' vigilante groups established to ensure patriotism. Others included the **Boy Spies of America,** the **American Defense Society,** and the **American Protective Association,** the largest with 250,000 members.

National War Labor Board (April 1918): American Federation of Labor President **Samuel Gompers** sat on this board, created by President Wilson to mediate labor disputes so that strikes would be avoided.
- Workers agreed not to strike, and employers pledged not to engage in lockouts.
- It also urged industry to implement changes that would benefit labor (e.g., an 8-hour day and the right of unions to organize and bargain collectively).

Sedition Act (May 1918): More repressive than the Espionage Act, it established punishment for interfering with the sale of Liberty Bonds, for writing or speaking against the government, the U.S. Constitution, the armed forces, or the flag and for impending recruitment efforts.

Overman Act (May 1918): Gave President Wilson almost dictatorial powers until 6 months after the war's end. These powers included the authority to reorganize executive agencies or create new ones.

Key 36 Postwar developments abroad

OVERVIEW *Even before the end of the war, Woodrow Wilson formulated his international philosophy, an idealistic vision based on principle. With the Senate's rejection of the Versailles Treaty, however, the United States failed to give its seal of approval to Wilson's new world order.*

Fourteen Points: Presented by President Wilson in an address to Congress on January 8, 1918, as the basis for peace terms at the close of World War I.
- Espoused a belief in the right of all peoples to self-determination, as evidenced by recommendations for boundary adjustments along with the creation of new nations.
- Included also: freedom of the seas, open covenants, adjustment of colonial claims with respect for native populations, free trade, reductions in armaments, and impartial mediation of colonial claims.
- Proposed a League of Nations, an association of nations that would aid in implementing the new principles and in resolving future controversies.

Paris Peace Conference: Held beginning in December 1918.
- Participants included **David Lloyd George,** prime minister of Great Britain, **Georges Clemenceau,** president of France, **Vittorio Orlando,** prime minister of Italy; and **Woodrow Wilson,** president of the United States.
- The conference formulated the general terms of the treaties ending World War I.

League of Nations: On January 25, 1919, at the Paris Peace Conference, the Allies voted to accept the creation of the League of Nations.
- This assembly of nations would oversee world affairs and prevent future wars.
- League decisions would be implemented by a nine-member Executive Council consisting of five permanent members: Britain, France, Italy, Japan, and the United States.
- The League was established in 1920, although the U.S. Senate rejected the treaty of which the League was a part.
- Although the United States did not formally join the League of Nations, it did take part in many of its activities.
- In 1946 the United Nations replaced the League of Nations.

Treaty of Versailles: Signed in June 1919, it was the peace treaty that ended World War I.

- In 1919 and again in 1920, the treaty failed to receive the necessary two-thirds approval of the Senate because it provided for the creation of the League of Nations. Senators **Henry Cabot Lodge, Hiram Johnson,** and **William E. Borah** were its strongest opponents.
- Finally, on August 25, 1921, a joint resolution declaring the war to be over was adopted by Congress.

Key 37 Postwar developments at home

OVERVIEW *The postwar years were marked by social unrest and violence in the United States. Economic problems, labor unrest, the fear of radicalism, and racial tensions had generated a sense of disillusionment.*

1919 and 1920 strikes: Raging inflation, concern about job security, and poor working conditions combined to generate labor discontent.
- In 1919 there were more than 3,600 strikes.
    1. A general strike in Seattle, Washington, nearly paralyzed the city, and U.S. Marines were sent in to keep it running.
    2. The National Guard was called in to restore order after the Boston Police Strike.
- The greatest single labor action at that time, which ended in failure, was the Great Steel Strike in January 1920, involving 350,000 steel-workers in several Midwestern states.

Red Scare (1919): Along with racial violence and labor unrest, the fear of revolution emerged. The Communist victory in the Russian Revolution of 1917 set these fears in motion.
- Established in 1919 in the Soviet Union, the Communist International sought to export revolution around the world.
- Americans began blaming revolutionaries or radical agitators for labor and racial disturbances.
- Hysteria mounted when a series of bombings occurred in the spring of 1919.
    1. The post office intercepted several packages addressed to leading politicians and businessmen, which were set to explode when opened.
    2. A few parcels did explode; in June 1919 eight bombs exploded in eight cities within minutes of one another.
    3. One bomb exploded outside the Washington townhouse of Attorney General **A. Mitchell Palmer.**

***Schenck* v. *United States* (1919):** Also reflecting the times was this Supreme Court decision involving Secretary Schenck of the Socialist Party, who was accused of distributing anti-draft literature during World War I.

- Justice Oliver Wendell Holmes stated that Schenck's First Amendment rights were not violated because free speech was never an absolute right, especially during wartime.
- Holmes declared that free speech does not permit an individual to yell fire in a crowded theater when there is none.

Palmer raids and other anti-Communist measures: As attorney general, Palmer set up an antiradical division in the Justice Department and appointed **J. Edgar Hoover,** a young government attorney, to direct what soon became the **Federal Bureau of Investigation (FBI).**
- In November 1919, the first attacks, known as "Palmer raids," were made on private homes of suspected Communist sympathizers and on headquarters of labor and radical organizations.
- In December 1919, the *U.S.S. Buford* left for Finland and the Soviet Union with 294 deported radicals.
- On January 1, 1920, 6,000 radicals were arrested as a result of the Palmer raids.
- Civil liberties were violated as citizens and aliens alike were denied legal counsel and held without specific charges.
- After May Day, 1920, had passed without any violence, the Red Scare soon abated.
- The summer of 1920 passed without major labor strikes or renewed bombings.

Sacco-Vanzetti case: A legacy of the Red Scare, the case began with the arrest in May 1920 of **Nicola Sacco** and **Bartolomeo Vanzetti** for murder in South Braintree, Massachusetts.
- Although the evidence against them was inadequate, as confessed anarchists they were presumed guilty.
- The judge in the trial was openly prejudiced.
- The two men were convicted, sentenced to death, and despite worldwide protests, executed in 1927.
- Many decades later, they were posthumously exonerated by Massachusetts Governor Michael Dukakis.

The great migration: During World War I, over half a million blacks migrated from the rural South to industrial cities in search of work.
- In 1917, race riots occurred in Houston, Philadelphia, and East St. Louis.
- In 1919 racial tension prevailed in the North and the South.
  1. More than 70 blacks died in lynchings in the South.
  2. In Chicago, white mobs attacked people, homes, and property in black neighborhoods. Thirty-eight people died and 537 were injured as blacks fought back.

Railroad Transportation Act (1920): Returned the railroads to private control and enlarged the **Interstate Commerce Commission** to 11 members.

- The act gave the commission authority to fix rates and to provide a 6 percent return, with half of all net earnings over this amount to be used for the benefit of weaker railroads.
- A **Railroad Board** was created to arbitrate disputes.

Water Power Act (1920): Created the **Federal Power Commission,** consisting of the secretaries of war, the interior, and agriculture, and authorized it to license the construction and operation of dams and hydroelectric plants on rivers and streams on public lands of the United States.

Theme 8 THE ROARING TWENTIES

*T*he 1920s were characterized by conservatism, afflu- ence, and cultural frivolity, yet it was also a time of social, economic, and political change. The first modern decade in American history paved the way for the reforms of the 1930s. American popular culture began to reflect an urban, industrial, consumer-oriented society. At the same time, conflicts surfaced regarding immigration restriction, Prohibition, and race relations. It was a transitional period in which consumption and leisure were replacing the older values of self-denial and the work ethic.

Key 38 The Republican era

OVERVIEW *For 12 years after 1921, the presidency and the Congress were controlled by Republicans. The federal government cultivated a relationship with American business. Despite its conservatism, the government experimented with new approaches to public policy and was an active agent of economic change.*

Election of 1920: The Republican candidate, **Warren G. Harding,** an obscure Ohio senator, defeated the Democratic candidate, Ohio Governor **James M. Cox,** and the Socialist Party candidate, **Eugene V. Debs.**
- The Republicans opposed U.S. admission to the League of Nations.
- The Republicans received 61 percent of the popular vote.

Warren G. Harding: Formerly a U.S. Senator from Ohio (1915–21), Harding served as president from 1921 until his unexpected death on August 2, 1923, in San Francisco while on a speaking tour.
- He helped streamline the budget, approved measures assisting farm cooperatives and liberalizing farm credit, supported antilynching legislation, and was tolerant on civil liberties issues.
- In 1921, he pardoned socialist Eugene V. Debs, who had been imprisoned during World War I for delivering a speech denouncing capitalism and the war.
- After his death, the Veterans Bureau and the Teapot Dome scandals (see below) overshadowed the administration of Calvin Coolidge, who succeeded Harding as president.

Ohio gang: These were certain friends of President Harding who, as government appointees, were responsible for the scandals of his administration. They included Charles R. Forbes, Harry M. Daughtery, Edwin Denby, and Albert B. Fall.

Veterans Bureau scandal (1923): A Senate investigation disclosed that **Charles R. Forbes,** director of the Veterans Bureau, was responsible for the waste and misappropriation of $250,000,000 of veterans' funds. He was found guilty and received a 2-year prison sentence and a $10,000 fine.

Teapot Dome (1924): One of the scandals of the Harding administration exposed by a 1924 congressional investigation, chaired by Senator

Thomas J. Walsh, involved naval oil reserves at Teapot Dome, Wyoming, and Elk Hills, California.

- In 1921, Secretary of the Interior **Albert B. Fall** encouraged Harding to transfer control of the reserves from the Navy Department to the Interior Department.
- Then Fall secretly leased the reserves to **Harry F. Sinclair** and **Edward L. Doheny** in return for over $100,000 in "loans."
- Charged with fraud and corruption, Fall was convicted of bribery and sentenced to 1 year in prison and a $100,000 fine.
- Sinclair and Doheny were acquitted in their trials for bribery, but Sinclair was later sentenced to 9 months in prison for contempt.
- In 1927 the oil leases were cancelled.

Harry Daugherty: Harding's Attorney General (1921–24), he resigned under pressure in 1924.

- He was found to be lax in prosecuting for graft in the Veterans Bureau and in enforcing prohibition laws.
- In 1927 he was tried for conspiracy but was acquitted.
- A close friend and aid to Attorney General Daughtery, **Jesse Smith,** was found to be taking bribes, and he committed suicide.

Edwin Denby: Harding's Secretary of the Navy (1921–24), he resigned in 1924 as a result of his part in the Teapot Dome scandal.

Calvin Coolidge: He completed President Harding's term (1923–25) and was then elected for a second term (1925–29).

- He had gained national prominence for his handling of the Boston police strike while serving as governor of Massachusetts (1919–20).
- He was an inactive president, proposing no significant legislation and avoiding foreign policy initiatives.
- Thus he acted on his belief that government should interfere as little as possible in the life of the nation.

Andrew Mellon (1921–29): As secretary of the treasury, he got Congress to cut taxes on corporate profits, personal incomes, and inheritances. He was also responsible for streamlining the federal budget and for reducing the nation's World War I debt.

Herbert Hoover (1921–28): As secretary of commerce under Harding and Coolidge, he worked to promote a more efficient, better organized national economy.

- Advocated "associational" activity for business.
- Believed that such trade associations, through shared information and active cooperation, would strengthen the economy.

Election of 1924: This contest was between incumbent **Calvin Coolidge,** a Republican, and a Wall Street lawyer, **John W. Davis,** a Democrat and former ambassador to Great Britain (1918–1921).

- **Robert LaFollette** ran on the Progressive ticket.
  1. Farmers and labor leaders had formed this third party, expressing discontent with the established parties.
  2. Progressives called for nationalization of the railroads, public ownership of utilities, direct election of the president, and the right of Congress to overrule Supreme Court decisions.
- Coolidge won easily.

Election of 1928: The Republican, Secretary of Commerce **Herbert C. Hoover,** defeated the Democratic candidate, Governor of New York **Alfred E. Smith,** the first Catholic candidate to run for president, and the Socialist Party candidate, **Norman Thomas.**

- Prohibition was a major campaign issue; Republicans supported it, and Democrats opposed it.
- Hoover received 58 percent of the popular vote.

Herbert Hoover (1929–33): As the Republican president from 1929 to 1933, his administration is generally associated with the **stock market crash** and the beginning of the **Great Depression.** At the end of his administration (1933) the **Twentieth Amendment,** which provides that presidents begin their terms in January, was passed.

KEY QUOTATION

Return to "normalcy."

Warren G. Harding (1920)
Republicans signal a return to prewar isolationism.

Key 39 Economic conditions

OVERVIEW *Throughout the 1920s farmers and labor organizations made few gains. After a recession in 1921–22, the gross national product grew by 40 percent, unemployment remained around 3 or 4 percent, and inflation was negligible. Farmers never rebounded after the recession and faced difficulties throughout the decade.*

Welfare capitalism: Paternalistic techniques adopted by industrial employers and designed to weaken the union movement and to remove the causes of industrial discontent.
- Workers received important economic benefits: bonuses, insurance plans, profit-sharing, and medical services.
- Welfare capitalism affected a relatively small number of workers and did not offer them real control over their working lives.

"American plan": Corporate leaders' crusade for the open shop, which received the support of the **National Association of Manufacturers** in 1920.
- Union busting prevailed in the 1920s because unions were viewed as un-American and subversive.
- Union power was curbed by actions of the Justice Department and the Supreme Court.
- Consequently, union membership seriously declined.

Norris-LaGuardia Act (1932): Prohibited the use of injunctions against certain union practices such as strikes, boycotts, and picketing.
- Made "yellow dog" contracts, those in which an employee agrees not to join a union, unenforceable in the courts.
- Guaranteed jury trials for strikers held for contempt of court.

Conditions among farmers: Primarily because of overproduction, food prices and farm income declined sharply during the 1920s. Many farmers lost ownership of their land and were forced to rent land from banks or landlords.

Emergency Tariff Act (1921): Raised the rates on agricultural products; overall, was designed to end the downward trend of tariff rates.

Fordney-McCumber Tariff (1922): Imposed the highest tariff rates in U.S. history.

- Rates were increased on farm products and on dyes, chemicals, hardware, toys, and lace.
- The president could change rates by as much as 50 percent on the recommendation of the Tariff Commission.

McNary-Haugen Bill (1924–28): This agricultural measure, which incorporated the idea of **parity** (a complex price-raising scheme), was introduced into Congress repeatedly between 1924 and 1928. It was sponsored by the **farm bloc,** a group of congressmen who supported bills to aid agriculture.

Grain and Cotton Stabilization Corporation (1930): Established by the **Federal Farm Board** and authorized to purchase grain and cotton in order to raise prices, the agency was unsuccessful because commodity prices did not remain at a high level.

Key 40 Material culture in America

OVERVIEW *The urban- and consumer-oriented culture affected the lives of Americans in the 1920s. This culture helped to homogenize American life, creating a new middle class. New values, reflecting economic prosperity, became increasingly prevalent. As millions of Americans began to share the same daily experiences, a national culture was born.*

Consumerism: Patterns of consumption and leisure made the 1920s a distinctive decade.
- Advertising and the movies fed the materialistic desires of the mass consumption economy. Whether rich or poor, Americans began purchasing goods for pleasure as well as for need.
- They bought appliances, commercially processed foods, mass-produced automobiles, cosmetics, and fashions.
- Consumption became a dominant cultural ideal, and with it came the introduction of **installment buying.**
  1. The installment plan was most often utilized to purchase an automobile.
  2. However, the "buy now, pay later" philosophy quickly spread to other items: radios, sewing machines, refrigerators.

Motion picture industry: A highly influential force in shaping popular culture because it promoted the diffusion of common values and attitudes nationwide.
- Movies were one of the main growth industries of the 1920s.
  1. Major film studios built elaborate movie palaces in most large cities.
  2. By 1930, national weekly movie attendance grew to 115 million.
- Movies with sound first appeared in 1927.
- Movies encouraged consumerism as well as new patterns of leisure and recreation.
- They created national trends in clothing and hair styles and even served as a form of sex education.

Radio: The newest instrument of mass culture during the 1920s.
- America's first commercial radio station, **KDKA** in Pittsburgh, began broadcasting in 1920.
- The **National Broadcasting Company,** the first national radio network, was established in 1927.

- Stations featured sports events, news, and variety entertainment shows and broadcast advertisements.
- By 1929, 40 percent of American households owned radios, with broadcasts linking the nation together by providing listeners with a common source of information and entertainment.
- The radio elevated professional sports to a national pastime and fueled American consumerism.

Leisure: Public recreation thrived as state and local governments built baseball diamonds, swimming pools, golf courses, and tennis courts. In the New York metropolitan area, for example, **Robert Moses** created a vast system of highways, parks, playgrounds, and picnic areas.

Sports: Professional sports flourished during the 1920s.
- Baseball drew about 10 million fans each year, truly becoming the national pastime.
- College football and boxing were exceedingly popular.
- Numerous sports heroes emerged at this time (e.g., **Gene Tunney, Babe Ruth, Red Grange, Bobby Jones, Bill Tilden**).
- **Gertrude Ederle,** who broke all records by swimming the English Channel in just over 14 hours in 1927, was the decade's best-known swimmer.

Jazz: A musical innovation of the decade, it sparked the term "the Jazz Age."
- It was brought from the South to northern cities such as Chicago and New York.
- Early jazz musicians were black: examples include **Ferdinand Morton** and **Louis Armstrong.**

The automobile: The most important symbol of the 1920s, it had a pervasive effect on every aspect of American life.
- It stimulated economic prosperity, affected patterns of crime, and shaped the sexual behavior of young men and women.
- Car ownership encouraged suburbanization, fueled real estate speculation, and promoted the development of shopping centers.
- The automobile also changed patterns of leisure as more Americans took to the roads (many unpaved) for day trips or extensive vacations.
- The **Ford Model T** was the most popular car of the decade. Fifteen million were mass-produced between 1908 and 1927, when the **Ford Model A** was introduced.

Key 41 American writers

OVERVIEW *Young American writers and intellectuals believed that materialism was overshadowing personal fulfillment.*

The lost generation: Young American writers and intellectuals who believed that the United States no longer furnished the means to achieve personal fulfillment.
- They felt alienated from modern society, which they characterized as cold, impersonal, and materialistic.
- Much of their disillusionment had its origin in the World War I experience.
- One of the most popular of this new breed of writers was **Ernest Hemingway,** whose novel *A Farewell to Arms* (1929) expressed his generation's contempt for the war.
- Other leading writers/critics included:
    1. **H. L. Mencken,** a Baltimore journalist who ridiculed American life in his magazines, *Smart Set* and *American Mercury.*
    2. **Sinclair Lewis,** the first American to win a Nobel Prize in literature. His satirical works include *Main Street, Babbitt, Elmer Gantry,* and *Arrowsmith.*
    3. **F. Scott Fitzgerald,** who critiqued the American obsession with material success in *The Great Gatsby* and explored the culture of youth in *This Side of Paradise.*
    4. **Eugene O'Neill,** the first great American playwright and the only one ever to win a Nobel Prize.

Southern intellectuals: Writers, referred to as "fugitives" and "agrarians," who evoked the strong rural traditions of their region. They attacked the growth and modernization of industrial society in a collection of essays, *I'll Take My Stand* (1930), advocating the South as a model for the rest of America.

Key 42 Women and blacks in the 1920s

OVERVIEW *While experiencing change, these groups were not part of the mainstream of prosperity during the decade.*

The new woman: Although the "new professional woman" was a widely publicized image of the 1920s, most working women were not professionals.
- The image of the "new woman" was characterized by the flapper, whose liberated lifestyle included smoking, drinking, dancing, wearing seductive clothes and makeup, and attending lively parties.
- Most middle-class women remained at home as housewives and mothers, with few combining marriage and a career.
- Married women were encouraged to think in terms of their own sexual fulfillment.

Women's activism: Reforming zeal and associational activity continued in the 1920s.
- The **Young Women's Christian Association (YWCA)** and **General Federation of Women's Clubs** expanded; the **League of Women Voters** and women's auxiliaries of the Republican and Democratic parties were organized.
- The **Equal Rights Amendment** was first introduced into Congress in 1923.
- The **Sheppard-Towner Act** (1921), although short-lived, provided federal funds to states to establish prenatal and child health care programs.
  1. It was a triumph for the Women's Joint Congressional Committee.
  2. This Washington coalition of 10 major women's organizations lobbied for reform legislation of interest to women.

Harlem renaissance: Black intellectuals created a thriving Afro-American culture in New York City's Harlem.
- Poets, novelists, artists, and musicians utilized their African roots to demonstrate the richness of their racial heritage.
- Examples include **Langston Hughes, James Weldon Johnson, Countee Cullen, Zora Neale Hurston, Claude McKay,** and **Alvin Locke.**

Marcus Garvey: Jamaican-born leader of a black working-class movement advocating a return to Africa.

- The movement published *Negro World,* a newspaper, and supported black capitalism through business ventures.
- It sponsored the **Black Star Line,** a steamship company to transport cargo between the United States and the West Indies, as well as American blacks to Africa.
- The movement collapsed when financial irregularities in raising money for the Black Star Line led to mail fraud indictments against Garvey and several associates.

KEY FIGURES

Margaret Sanger: A public health nurse, she led the **national birth control movement,** advocating the use of contraceptive devices, particularly the diaphragm.

Marcus Garvey: Claiming 4 million members, his **Universal Negro Improvement Association,** based in Harlem, advocated black migration back to Africa, alleging mistreatment by white-ruled nations.

Key 43 Response to the new culture

OVERVIEW *Alongside the modern, secular, new culture of the 1920s was the older, traditional culture of Americans living in small towns and farming communities. Most of these people both resented and feared the secular values of the urban-based, mass-consumption society. Their conservative outlook precipitated several cultural controversies during the decade as they sought to protect their cultural, economic, and political lifestyle.*

Immigration Act of 1921: Limited immigration from European, Australian, Near Eastern, and African countries.
- Immigration was limited to 3 percent of the total number of persons of each of these nationalities residing in the United States, based on the 1910 census.
- The maximum number to be admitted in any one year was 357,803 people from all countries.

Cable Act (1922): Made changes in the naturalization laws.
- An alien woman could no longer acquire automatic U.S. citizenship by marrying a U.S. citizen.
- A woman who was a citizen would not lose her citizenship if she married an alien.

Immigration Act of 1924: Limited the number of immigrants admitted to the United States in any one year to 164,000.
- European immigration was limited to 2 percent of the total number of each nationality residing in the United States, based on the 1890 census.
- Immigration from East Asia was banned.

National Origins Act (1929): Limited the total number of immigrants admitted to the United States in any one year to 150,000. Quotas were allotted to various European nations on the basis of the number of each nationality living in the United States, based on the 1920 census.

Ku Klux Klan: A prime example of nativism in the 1920s, the modern Klan targeted Catholics, Jews, and foreigners as well as blacks.
- However, because it also sought to defend traditional culture against modern values and morals, it attacked persons guilty of sexual promiscuity or drunkenness, and those lacking religious values.

- This new Klan had emerged in 1915 in Georgia under the leadership of **William J. Simmons.**
- The Klan had 4 million members in 1925, from both rural and urban areas.
- Internal scandals and a changing national climate were responsible for its decline after 1925.

Fundamentalism: This movement, promoted by provincial men and women, generally from rural America, sought to preserve and maintain traditional religion as the center of American life.
- Fundamentalists believed in a literal interpretation of the Bible and opposed the evolutionary theories of **Charles Darwin.**
- In 1925, for example, it became illegal in Tennessee for any public school teacher to each evolution. This law led to the famous **Scopes** or **"monkey" trial.**
  1. Promised free counsel by the American Civil Liberties Union to any Tennessee teacher willing to defy the law, **John T. Scopes,** a 24-year-old biology teacher, had himself arrested.
  2. The trial, which featured **William J. Bryan** as the prosecutor and **Clarence Darrow** as the defense attorney, attracted international attention and was broadcast on radio.
  3. Scopes was convicted and fined but the fine was remitted by the Tennessee Supreme Court.
  4. Bryan, who had been made to appear foolish as he asserted his faith in biblical teachings, died soon after the trial.

Prohibition: The **Eighteenth Amendment** prohibited the manufacture, transport, or sale of liquor after January 16, 1920.
- While rural Protestant Americans defended the amendment, it became a factor in organized crime in major cities. Al Capone's criminal empire in Chicago was built largely on illegal alcohol.
- The government hired only 1,500 agents to enforce Prohibition, and ordinary people defied the law; many made "bathtub gin" at home.
- Churches could still use wine for sacramental purposes, and doctors could prescribe alcohol for medicinal reasons.
- Although Prohibition caused a temporary decline in drinking, particularly in beer consumption during the 1920s, the legislation was a failure.
- The Eighteenth Amendment was repealed on December 5, 1933.

Key 44 Foreign policy of the 1920s

OVERVIEW *After World War I, the United States was eager to support political and economic stability abroad while keeping free of commitments that would limit its freedom of action. American foreign policy was one of "moral cooperation," consisting of agreements to control arms and unofficial support for private financial arrangements aimed at preventing international economic collapse. Such limited internationalism did not protect vital self-interests of the United States or create global stability.*

Washington Naval Conference (1921–22): Initiated by Secretary of State Charles Evans Hughes, it attempted to prevent a naval arms race among the United States, Britain, and Japan.
- These three nations, along with France, Italy, Belgium, Portugal, the Netherlands, and China, met in Washington.
- Three treaties resulted:
    1. **The Five-Power Pact (1922):** The United States, Great Britain, Japan, Italy, and France agreed to a 10-year naval holiday during which time no new ships would be built. Limits for total naval tonnage were established as well: for every 5 tons of American and British warships, Japan would maintain 3 and France and Italy, 1.75 each.
    2. **The Nine-Power Pact:** It pledged to maintain China's territorial integrity and independence and to support the "open door" policy.
    3. **The Four-Power Pact:** The United States, Britain, France, and Japan agreed to respect each other's rights in their Pacific island possessions and pledged to settle disputes concerning these areas by joint negotiation.

Geneva Naval Disarmament Conference (1927): Initiated by President Coolidge to consider limitations on the construction of smaller naval craft, it was attended only by Japan, Great Britain, and the United States. No agreement was reached in extending the restrictions agreed upon at the Washington Conference.

London Naval Conference (1930): The Five-Power Pact was expanded to cover a full range of warships.

Kellogg-Briand Pact (1928): Negotiated by French Foreign Minister **Aristide Briand** and Secretary of State **Frank Kellogg,** who received the Nobel Peace Prize in 1929, this multilateral treaty outlawed war as an instrument of national policy.
- Initially signed by 14 nations, later by 48 others.
- Made no provision for enforcement, other than the "moral force" of world opinion.

Dawes Plan (1924): After World War I, European nations owed debts of about $26 billion. The ability of the Allies to repay the United States depended upon Germany's ability to pay its war debts to the Allies.
- By 1923–24, Germany began to default on its debts, while experiencing runaway inflation.
- French troops subsequently occupied the Ruhr.
- An American banker, **Charles Dawes,** negotiated large private loans from American banks to revive the German economy.
- Under his plan, Britain and France would agree to reduce the amount of Germany's reparations over a 5-year period.
- For his work, Dawes shared the Nobel Peace Prize with **Sir Joseph Austin Chamberlain** in 1925.

Young Plan (1929): Reformulated the Dawes Plan to manage future war debts and reparations.
- Created by a committee headed by **Owen D. Young,** a banker and industrialist, the plan provided for reducing Germany's reparations to $8,000,000,000.
- It allowed payment to be made over the next 59 years.

War-debt moratorium: When the depression in Europe affected the European nations' ability to repay their debts to the United States, President Hoover in 1931 declared a 1-year moratorium on the payment of war debts.

Lusanne Conference (1932): Resulted in an Allied agreement that future reparations and debt payments by Germany were impossible but that Germany should make one last payment. The United States rejected the plan because it made no provision for debt payments to the United States by the Allies.

The World Court: Under Presidents Harding, Coolidge, and Hoover, proposals for U.S. membership in the World Court were defeated by the Senate. In 1926 the Senate attached so many special conditions to America's participation in the World Court that the court itself rejected America's admission.

Latin American Policy: The United States intervened in Latin American affairs to protect its interests.

- In 1924, U.S. troops left the Dominican Republic, but Americans supervised government finances there until 1940.
- In 1926, Coolidge sent marines into Nicaragua to police a national election and quell disturbances.
- In 1928, Coolidge sent **Dwight Morrow,** a skillful negotiator, to Mexico City to formulate compromises that quieted the concerns of U.S. corporations involved in Mexico's oil industry. Mexico's 1917 Constitution had claimed all subsoil wealth as the property of the Mexican people.
- Colombia received a $25 million indemnity from the United States for its loss of Panama in 1921.
- In 1930, the **Clark Memorandum,** which repudiated Roosevelt's Corollary justifying unilateral intervention in Latin American countries, was issued.

Hoover-Stimson Doctrine (1932): Stating that the United States would refuse to recognize any treaty that impaired the sovereignty of China or infringed on the "open door" policy, the doctrine was enunciated as a response to the 1931 Japanese invasion of Manchuria. By 1932, Manchuria had become the Japanese puppet state of Manchukuo.

Theme 9 THE GREAT DEPRESSION AND THE NEW DEAL

*T*he U.S. economy virtually collapsed over the 3 years following the stock market crash. The Great Depression continued throughout the 1930s until World War II brought American prosperity. Under the leadership of a new Democratic president, Franklin Delano Roosevelt, the New Deal program for economic relief, recovery, and reform expanded the federal presence in the economy and guaranteed a wide range of social and economic benefits to Americans. The New Deal initiated a limited welfare state and restored confidence in the capitalist economic system.

INDIVIDUAL KEYS IN THIS THEME

Key 45 Origins of the Great Depression

OVERVIEW *While the stock market crash of 1929 was the first sign of the Great Depression, other factors explain why this depression was so severe and why it lasted so long. A flawed stock market was only one economic weakness.*

Lack of diversification: The U.S. economy's prosperity depended upon a few basic industries, particularly construction and automobiles.
- At the end of the 1920s, these industries began to decline.
- The newer petroleum, chemical, and plastic industries were not strong enough to compensate.

Maldistribution of purchasing power: The proportion of profits from industrial and agricultural production going to farmers, workers, and other consumers was too small to create an adequate market, resulting in low consumer demand versus an ever-increasing supply.
- In 1929 over half of U.S. families were too poor to buy basic necessities, houses, or cars.
- The auto and construction industries reduced their work forces, further limiting purchasing power.

Banks and the credit structure: Throughout the 1920s, farmers were in debt. Their land was mortgaged, and crop prices were too low to allow them to pay off debts to banks.
- The banking system was inadequately prepared to absorb a major recession.
- Small banks, many tied to the agricultural sector of the economy, experienced failures as many debtors defaulted on loans.
- The Federal Reserve system only loosely regulated the banking system.
- Some larger banks maintained inadequate reserves against stock market investments and had made unwise loans.

America's position in international trade: During the 1920s, exports were a significant factor in the U.S. economy.
- However, demand for American goods declined by the end of the decade when European industry and agriculture improved.
- Foreign nations were experiencing their own financial crises.
- Decline in demand also involved the international debt structure, which destabilized the European economy.

International debt structure: European nations that had been aligned with the United States during World War I owed large amounts of money to American banks.

- This was one reason why reparation payments from Germany and Austria were imposed; it was thought that such payments would help France and Britain to pay off their American debts.
- In spite of the faltering economies of European nations, the United States refused to forgive or reduce debts incurred by European nations.
- Still greater debts were incurred when American banks made larger loans to European countries.
  1. When the American economy weakened after 1929, it became more difficult for these nations to borrow from the United States.
  2. High protective tariffs in America made it difficult for European nations to sell their products in American markets.
  3. They began to default on their loans due to these factors.
- After 1931, the Great Depression spread to Europe as a result of the collapse of this international debt structure.

Stock market crash (October 1929): Caused by overspeculation in stocks, expansion in some industries, and overproduction of agricultural products, followed by deflated prices, easy credit, and the collapse of the market overseas.

- By 1932, stock market values were one-tenth of the 1929 values.
- The slump continued until the market dropped below prewar levels during the summer of 1932.

Panic of 1929: Set off by the stock market crash in October.

- Causes included overspeculation in stocks, overextension of loans, and the inflationary trend that had begun in 1924.
- Effects included widespread unemployment, bank closings, and mortgaged foreclosures.

KEY FIGURE

Andrew W. Mellon: Secretary of the treasury under Coolidge and Hoover, he supported the "trickle down" theory of economics, whereby government reduces taxes on corporate profits and personal incomes to stimulate the economy.

Key 46 American society faces the Great Depression

OVERVIEW *American society was deeply affected by the Great Depression. By 1932 about one-fourth of the work force was unemployed, and throughout the decade unemployment remained about 20 percent. The American banking system collapsed and the total money supply fell, resulting in a decline in purchasing power and terrible deflation.*

Unemployment: With thousands unemployed, many families were thrown into turmoil.
- Many sought assistance from public relief systems and private charities, both of which were unable to handle the high demand.
- Others took to the roads as nomads in search of work.
- Many farmers, both black and white, also left their homes because their produce or crops could be sold only at prices so low as to make farming unprofitable.
  1. In particular, many families from the Dust Bowl, the southern part of the Great Plains, became migrant farmworkers.
  2. Their land had been devastated by extensive farming, deforestation, droughts, and soil erosion.
- Homelessness and malnutrition, the results of unemployment, permeated both urban and rural America.

Effect on middle-class families: The economic hardships of the Great Depression had the greatest impact on middle-class families.
- Rural families, black families, and migrant families were more accustomed to coping with adverse circumstances.
- In middle-class urban families, marriage and birth rates declined during the decade, along with the divorce rate.
- Informal breakups of families occurred as unemployed men left their households, On the other hand, many households expanded to include relatives.
- The family's consumer habits changed. Unable to purchase many items, women sewed clothes and preserved food.
- Some engaged in home businesses; by taking in laundry, accepting boarders, or selling baked goods, women helped their families survive.

Culture: The ideals of work and individual advancement survived the Great Depression.
- A best-selling book of the time was **Dale Carnegie's** *How to Win Friends* and *Influence People* (1936).
  1. It preached personal initiative as the route to success.
  2. However, it also conveyed the idea that the best way for people to make something of themselves was to adapt to their world by understanding the values and expectations of others and by molding themselves accordingly.
- American artists and writers portrayed the suffering of rural and urban folk.
  1. Photographers such as **Roy Stryker** and **Dorothea Lange** recorded agricultural life.
  2. **Erskine Caldwell** and **James Agee** wrote about southern life.
  4. **Richard Wright** dealt with the urban ghetto, while **James Farrell** described the world of urban, lower-class white youth.
  4. In *The Grapes of Wrath* (1939) **John Steinbeck** portrayed the trials of a migrant family in California.
- Other writers, such as **John Dos Passos** and **Clifford Odets,** focused on political themes.
- Amid the economic suffering, there was a need for escapism.
  1. For the most part, radio and movies provided light entertainment, particularly comedies and musicals.
  2. **Margaret Mitchell's** *Gone With the Wind* (1936), a Civil War saga, was one of the most celebrated films of the period.

Radicalism: Small numbers of intellectuals, artists, workers, and blacks became involved in radical causes during the Great Depression.
- Some became members of, or sympathizers with, the American Communist Party.
- Others formed the **Abraham Lincoln Brigade** and traveled to Spain to fight in the Spanish Civil War.
- Aside from creating and directing the brigade, the Communist Party was a major force in organizing unions and advocating racial justice.
- While socialism never became a major force in the politics of the decade, the **Southern Tenant Farmer's Union,** supported by the Socialist Party and organized by **H. L. Mitchell,** tried to establish a biracial coalition of sharecroppers, tenant farmers, and others demanding economic reform.

Key 47 Impact of the Great Depression
on minorities and women

OVERVIEW *The New Deal failed to eradicate racism and sexism from American society. For both minorities and women the social and economic gains were limited.*

Blacks: Unemployment, homelessness, malnutrition and disease affected black Americans to a greater degree than most whites.
- Intimidation and violence were often used to drive blacks from jobs.
- Relief went to whites before blacks, and some public and private charities refused any assistance to blacks.
- Some rural blacks migrated to southern cities, but many more journeyed north.
- Overall, lynching, segregation, and disfranchisement in the South remained unchallenged.
- However, the **National Association for the Advancement of Colored People (NAACP)** gained a place for blacks in the emerging labor movement.
- **The Scottsboro Case:** Nine black teenagers were taken off a freight train in Alabama and arrested for vagrancy and disorder.
  1. Two white women on the train then accused them of rape.
  2. Although there was no evidence of their guilt, an all-white jury in Alabama convicted all nine and sentenced eight to death.
  3. In 1932 the convictions were overturned by the Supreme Court, and new trials continued during the 1930s.
  4. All nine finally gained their freedom; charges were dropped for four, four received early paroles, and one escaped.

Hispanics: Like blacks, Mexican and Mexican-Americans faced discrimination during the Great Depression.
- As farmers, menial workers, and agricultural migrants, they largely inhabited the Southwest and California.
- Like blacks, they were the last to be hired and the first to be fired.
- Many left for Mexico in search for work.
- Others migrated to cities such as Los Angeles, where they lived in urban poverty.
- Most relief programs excluded them, and schools and hospitals denied them access.

Women: The Great Depression bolstered the belief that a woman's place was in the home.

- Most people believed that available work should go to men.
- In fact, from 1932 to 1937 it was illegal for more then one member of a family to hold a federal civil service job.
- Nevertheless, because their families needed to survive, 25 percent more women (often wives and mothers) worked during the 1930s than in previous years.
- Women professionals and industrial workers faced limited opportunities during the decade.
- The clerical field remained open, however, since men were unlikely to do such work.
- As in previous decades, black women were more likely to work than white women, although their choice of occupations was even more limited.

Key 48   Herbert Hoover's role in the crisis

OVERVIEW *President Hoover's response to the Great Depression at first involved encouragement of associationalism. When voluntary cooperation failed, he used federal action to stimulate the economy. Although his actions were on an unprecedented scale when compared with those of previous presidents, his programs proved to be too little too late.*

Volunteerism: To reverse the Great Depression, Hoover met with leaders of business, labor, and agriculture and urged them to maintain wages and production. He also implored labor leaders to forgo demands for higher wages and better hours.

Hawley-Smoot Tariff (1930): An attempt to protect American farmers from international competition by raising agricultural tariffs.
- Rates were raised to a new high of 50 percent.
- Rates on manufactured goods were also raised, making imported industrial products more expensive for farmers.
- In response, foreign governments enacted their own restrictions of trade, thus decreasing foreign demand for U.S. goods.

Revenue Act of 1932: The largest peacetime tax increase up to that time.
- Represented Hoover's response to the Federal Reserve's contraction on the money supply.
- Designed to raise revenues by one-third and to balance the budget.
- In practice, impeded consumption and investment.

Glass-Steagall Banking Act (1932): Made government securities available to back Federal Reserve notes.
- Countered credit contractions from gold withdrawals.
- Temporarily aided the ailing banking system.

Reconstruction Finance Corporation (1932): Lent money to banks, railroad companies, agricultural associations, and insurance companies in an effort to revive the economy and stop deflation.
- During the New Deal, financed many relief and recovery agencies.
- Was the first federal institution set up to intervene directly in the economy during peacetime, but its cautiousness in lending money limited its impact.
- Ended its operations in 1954.

Home Loan Bank Act (1932): Passed to encourage new home construction and reduce foreclosures.
- A board to control the operation of 12 Federal Home Loan banks was created.
- These banks extended credit to member banks and loan associations, whose chief business was in real estate development and home mortgages.

Bonus army march (1932): In June 1932, over 20,000 unemployed veterans marched on Washington, D.C., petitioning Congress to make immediate payment of a bonus to all who had served in World War I.
- Congress had approved a bonus in 1924, but the money was to be distributed in 1945.
- The "bonus army" built crude camps around the city.
- After Congress had voted down the veterans' appeal, President Hoover ordered the National Guard and the Army to remove the camps.
- Generals **Douglas MacArthur** and **George S. Patton** were involved in the removal process.

Farm Holiday Association (1932): An organization formed by a group of unhappy farmers in Des Moines, Iowa.
- Under the leadership of **Milo Reno,** they advocated withholding farm products from the market and a farmers' strike.
- Their efforts were too localized to be effective.

Election of 1932: This contest pitted Republican **Herbert Hoover** against Democrat **Franklin Delano Roosevelt,** who had been a New York State legislator, assistant secretary of the navy under Wilson, a vice-presidential candidate in 1920, and a two-term governor of New York.
- Roosevelt was more energetic, imaginative, and charismatic than Hoover and promised the American people a new deal.
- He portrayed the Great Depression as a domestic (and Republican) problem, while Hoover insisted that it was international in origin.
- Roosevelt received 57 percent of the popular vote.

Key 49 Roosevelt and the
New Deal philosophy

OVERVIEW *Franklin D. Roosevelt succeeded in restoring hope and confidence. His New Deal was not a carefully formulated plan, but offered a pragmatic and experimental approach incorporating relief, recovery, and reform measures.*

The "hundred days": Between March 9 and June 16, 1933, a special session of Congress enacted a series of laws dealing with the banking crisis and other conditions resulting from the Great Depression.

The "brain trust": This group of special advisors assisted President Roosevelt in developing a program for reconstructing the country; members included **Rexford G. Tugwell, Raymond Moley,** and **Adolphe A. Berle, Jr.**

Fireside chats: In these talks Roosevelt explained various New Deal projects.
- The first fireside chat took place on March 12, 1933.
- These broadcasts built public confidence in Roosevelt's administration.
- Roosevelt was the first president to make regular use of the radio.

Roosevelt's cabinet: Members included:
- A close friend and neighbor from Hyde Park, **Henry Morgenthau,** who served as secretary of the treasury; former Republican **Henry A. Wallace,** who became secretary of agriculture, and **Harold Ickes,** who became secretary of the interior.
- From his New York administration, Roosevelt brought the first woman to hold a cabinet post, **Frances Perkins,** who became secretary of labor.

Relief, recovery, reform: The programs that Roosevelt proposed encompassed three goals:
- *Relief:* provide immediate help to the poor and unemployed.
- *Recovery:* bring business back from the depths of bankruptcy.
- *Reform:* introduce into the economic system long-range changes that would prevent future depressions.

Key 50 Economic changes in the New Deal

OVERVIEW *President Roosevelt moved quickly to shore up the economy by supporting collapsing banks, and then proceeded to safeguard the economy though government involvement.*

Bank holiday: On March 6, 1933, President Roosevelt, by proclamation, declared a 4-day national banking holiday by suspending all transactions of banking institutions.
- Expert teams were sent out to classify every bank as strong, wavering, or hopeless.
- Over a billion dollars, from the **Reconstruction Finance Corporation (RFC),** was pumped into the banking system.

Emergency Banking Act (1933): Provided for the reopening of banks under supervision of the Federal Reserve and permitted that RFC to purchase stock in the national banks.
- Also prohibited gold hoarding and export.
- Gave Roosevelt emergency powers to regulate credit, currency, and foreign exchange.

Economy Act (1933): Designed to instill confidence in the federal government, it lowered government salaries by about 15 percent, reduced pension payments, and made changes in government agencies.

Glass-Steagall Banking Act (1933): Separated commercial and investment banking and restricted the use of bank credit for speculative purposes.
- Allowed national banks to establish branch banks.
- Expanded the **Federal Reserve system.**
- Set up the **Federal Deposit Insurance Corporation,** insuring bank deposits up to $2,500.

Truth in Securities Act (1933): Required that all corporation securities offered for interstate sale be registered with the **Federal Trade Commission,** along with full and accurate information about the corporation and its officers.

Securities and Exchange Commission (1934): Created to police the stock market.

- It could regulate the purchase of stocks on credit and restrict speculation of stocks on credit and restrict speculation by people with inside information on corporate plans.
- Market manipulation devices were prohibited.
- Corporations were required to publish all facts on their securities.
- Stock exchanges were licensed and required to list all securities that they trade.

Silver Purchase Act (1934): Designed to increase the price of silver and to strengthen the economy, it provided for the purchase of silver by the U.S. Treasury until the total value of such silver reached one-third the value of the government's gold stock, or until the price of silver reached $1.29 per ounce.

Gold Reserve Act (1934): Enabled the president to fix the devaluation of the dollar at 50 to 60 cents in relation to its gold content, purchase all gold stock in Federal Reserve banks, and place it in the U.S. Treasury, setting up a fund to stabilize the dollar.

Reciprocity Trade Agreement Act (1934): Authorized the president to negotiate agreements with other nations and reduce U.S. tariff rates by as much as 50 percent in return for lower foreign tariffs on U.S. exports.

Export-Import Bank (1934): Created to make loans or guarantee loans to private sources for the encouragement of foreign trade.

Revenue Wealth Tax Act (1935): Income tax rates remained unchanged, but surtaxes on net incomes ranged from 31 percent on incomes of $50,000 to 75 percent on incomes over $5 million.
- The federal estate tax was increased to a maximum of 70 percent.
- A graduated tax was levied on net corporation income.

Banking Act (1935): Represented a significant consolidation of federal control of the country's banks.
- Authorized the president to appoint a new board of governors of the Federal Reserve system.
- Placed control of interest rates and other money policies at the federal level.
- Encouraged centralization of the banking system by requiring all large state banks to join the Federal Reserve system by 1942.

Key 51 New Deal programs to assist people

OVERVIEW *Federal regulation extended over new areas of the economy, especially agriculture. The modern welfare state emerged, and the labor movement was supported by government policy.*

Home Owners Loan Corporation (1933): Created to provide funds to be used in refinancing first mortgages, at low interest rates, on homes evaluated at less than $20,000; money was lent and new long-term mortgages were arranged.

Federal Emergency Relief Act (1933): Established the **Federal Emergency Relief Administration (FERA),** headed by **Harry Hopkins,** which gave cash grants to states to bolster state relief agencies.

Civil Works Administration (1933): Provided work relief for over 4 million unemployed men.
- Created after it was evident that FERA grants were insufficient to sustain the needy.
- Developed one-time projects, such as the construction of roads, schools, and parks.

Emergency Relief Appropriations Act (1935): Created the **Works Progress Administration (WPA),** led by **Harry Hopkins,** as the main federal relief agency from 1935 to 1943.
- Directed the spending of federal funds for work relief projects.
- Included highway construction, flood control, reforestation, housing and slum clearance, and rural electrification, as well as educational, health, and sanitation projects.

Social Security Act (August 1935): A significant piece of social welfare legislation that created many programs.
- The act provided for old age, survivors', and disability insurance.
- It established a system of unemployment compensation.
- Employers and employees contributed to the pension system, which began in 1942, by paying a payroll tax.
- Initially many categories of workers were excluded from the program.

Agricultural Adjustment Act (1933): Allowed the secretary of agriculture to make subsidy payments to farmers who reduced their production of cotton, wheat, corn, rice, tobacco, and diary products.
- Farm prices were subsidized up to the point of parity.
- A processing tax on the commodities involved would cover the cost of such payments.
- Amended legislation added beets, cane sugar, barley, peanuts, rye, flax, beef, and dairy cattle to the list of items eligible for benefit payments.

Farm Credit Act (1933): Created the **Farm Credit Administration**, which lent money to farmers at low interest rates to halt foreclosures on farms; all farm credit agencies were placed under its control.

Commodity Credit Corporation (1933): Authorized loans to farmers for crops stored on their farms or in warehouses. The objective was to stabilize prices and bring about more orderly marketing practices.

Tennessee Valley Authority (1933): Charted by Congress and given the authority to acquire, construct, and operate dams, manufacture and distribute nitrate and fertilizer, generate and sell electric power, assist in rural electrification, help control floods, reclaim land, prevent soil erosion, and improve economic and social conditions. Its benefits extended to seven southern states.

Rural Electrification Administration (1935): Introduced electric service to rural areas without electricity. Long-term loans were granted for construction of power lines and for the wiring of farm buildings.

Resettlement Administration (1935): This agency and its successor, the Farm Security Administration, established in 1937, attempted, through loans, to help farmers cultivate submarginal soil and resettle on better land.

Civilian Conservation Corps (1933): Established to provide employment for 500,000 men.
- Projects involved reforestation, road construction, prevention of soil erosion, and irrigation.
- A series of camps was created in national parks and forests in which young men labored in a semimilitary environment.

Public Works Administration (1933): Established under NIRA and headed by Secretary of the Interior **Harold L. Ickes,** it promoted work relief by distributing money for public works programs. It received $3.3 billion for the construction, repair, or improvement of public buildings, roads, and other projects.

Support for literature and the arts: Under the WPA, four projects were included:

- The **Federal Writers Project** offered unemployed writers support for their own projects, as well as those initiated by the WPA.
- The **Federal Arts Project** employed artists, sculptors, and painters who produced work for schools, hospitals, and government buildings.
- The **Federal Music Project** provided employment for musicians.
- The **Federal Theater Project** produced concerts, plays, and skits, providing work for unemployed actors and directors.

National Industrial Recovery Act (NIRA) (1933): Created the **National Recovery Administration,** headed by **Hugh S. Johnson,** a retired general and businessman.

- The act set up a system of industrial self-government by drawing up codes of fair trade practices for each industry.
- These codes also established working conditions and abolished child labor.
- Under section 7(A), workers could form unions and engage in collective bargaining.

National Labor Relations Act (July 1935): Also known as the **Wagner Act,** it established the **National Labor Relations Board.**

- The board was authorized to investigate unfair labor practices and to issue cease and desist orders.
- The board was also empowered to supervise elections to determine the bargaining agent for all the employees in a business.

Wheeler-Howard Act (Indian Reorganization Act) (1935): Ended the program of distributing Indian tribal lands on an individual basis.

- Native Americans were now encouraged to reorganize on a tribal basis.
- The government offered them loans for soil improvement, irrigation, and land purchase.

Key 52 New Deal critics

OVERVIEW *After 2 years in office, Franklin D. Roosevelt became the target of public criticism as the Great Depression continued.*

American Liberty League (1934): Composed of wealthy Northern industrialists and conservative Democrats (about 125,000 members), led by the DuPont family.
- Opposed the New Deal's attacks on free enterprise and its "dictatorial" policies.

Dr. Francis E. Townsend: An elderly California physician who attracted more than 5 million members with his plan.
- The **Townsend plan,** founded in 1933, proposed paying pensions of $200 per month to all unemployed persons over 60.
- Funds for these payments would be provided by a 2 percent tax on business transactions.

Father Charles E. Coughlin: A Catholic priest in Royal Oak, Michigan, a Detroit suburb, who organized the **National Union for Social Justice,** which promoted his views.
- This organization supported remonetization of silver, issuing of greenbacks, and the nationalization of the banking system to restore prosperity and ensure economic justice.
- He became known as the **"radio priest"** because of his weekly sermons, broadcast nationally.

Huey Long: Was governor and senator from Louisiana and had presidential ambitions.
- He proposed the **share-our-wealth plan.**
  1. All incomes over $1 million and all inheritances over $5 million would be taxed.
  2. The money would be dispensed to all Americans.
  3. The government would acquire enough assets to guarantee every family a minimum "homestead" of $5,000 and an annual income of $2,500.
- The **Share-Our-Wealth Society,** created in 1935 as a national organization, had about 4 million members in 1935.
- Long's assassination in 1935 ended his presidential ambitions.

Key 53 End of the New Deal

OVERVIEW *Although President Roosevelt was at the height of his popularity in 1936, his second term was marked by continuing opposition, major economic setbacks, and his own political errors, particularly his court-packing plan.*

Election of 1936: Running against **Alfred M. Landon,** the Republican governor of Kansas (1933–37), and **William Lemke** of North Dakota, nominated by the Union Party formed by **Coughlin, Townsend,** and **Long** supporters, Roosevelt received almost 61 percent of the popular vote.
- While Democrats defended the New Deal, Republicans criticized the inefficiency and expense of many of its programs.
- The Democrats also won majorities in both houses of Congress.

"Court-packing plan": This judiciary reorganization bill was submitted to Congress in February 1937, by Roosevelt.
- It proposed to appoint an additional member of the Supreme Court for each one over 70 years of age.
- It was a response to the Court's invalidation of the **National Recovery Administration** *(Schecter* v. *United States)* **and the Agricultural Adjustment Act** *(United States* v. *Butler).*
- It was never approved by Congress because it was viewed as an attempt by the president to fill the court with justices who would approve New Deal legislation.
- Meanwhile, the **Wagner Act** *(National Labor Relations Board* v. *Jones & Laughlin Steel Corporation)* and the **Social Security Act** were validated by the Supreme Court in 1937.
- A rapid sequence of deaths and retirements between 1937 and 1941 enabled Roosevelt to select seven associate justices and a chief justice.

Recession of 1937: Began in the fall of 1937 and lasted for 9 months.
- The Federal Reserve Board tightened credit by raising interest rates, and budgets were cut for relief programs.
- Recovery began in 1938 after $5 billion was appropriated by Congress for relief and for public works programs.

Bankhead-Jones Farm Tenancy Act (1937): Created the **Farm Security Administration,** which was authorized to extend low-interest-rate loans, repayable in small installments, to farm tenants and sharecroppers.

- The money was to be used to purchase new land.
- The act provided also for rehabilitation loans and assistance to migrant workers.

Fair Labor Standards Act (1938): Established a minimum wage (40 cents/hour initially), a maximum work week of 40 hours, and an official rate of time-and-a-half for overtime work, and abolished child labor in industries producing goods for interstate commerce.

"New" Agricultural Adjustment Act (1938): Designed to replace the Agricultural Adjustment Act of 1933, declared unconstitutional in 1936.
- The secretary of agriculture was authorized to limit acreages planted in crops and to control the marketing of surplus crops.
- Farmers were to be paid for limiting crops and practicing soil conservation.
- Storage facilities were provided to maintain an "ever-normal granary."

House Un-American Activities Committee (May 1938): Investigated, under chairman **Martin Dies** of Texas, liberal groups, labor leaders, New Dealers, and Communists.
- The committee was looking for evidence of their involvement in subversive activities.
- Of nearly 3,800 government employees it recommended for dismissal, only 36 warranted this action.

Key 54 Impact and legacy of the
New Deal

OVERVIEW *The New Deal preserved corporate capitalism by grafting a limited welfare state onto a capitalist
foundation. Although it did establish clearly government
involvement in regulating the economy, it did not radically
redistribute income.*

Impact of the New Deal: It did not end the Great Depression, but did
prevent further decay of the economy.
• Established a safety net for various groups who suffered economically and made America a more humane industrial society.
• Encouraged farmers and workers to challenge the power of
corporations.

Legacy of the New Deal: Economy was stabilized through the
increased regulatory functions of the federal government.
• Created the basis for new forms of federal fiscal policy.
  1. Federal legislation more tightly regulating the stock market and
     the Federal Reserve System was formed.
  2. Many practices of modern corporate life became subject to fed-
     eral regulation.
• Created an American welfare state in which the federal commitment to citizens' economic security grew.
• Expanded presidential power and enhanced the power of the federal government.
• Increased the growth of the federal bureaucracy.
• Created a Democratic Party coalition that would dominate American politics for many years. It included ethnic groups, city
  dwellers, organized labor, blacks, as well as a broad section of the
  middle class.
• Awakened voter interest in economic matters, and increased
  expectations of government accomplishments.

The "broker state": The New Deal made the federal government a pro-
tector of interest groups and a mediator of the competition among
them.
• These interest groups initially involved the labor movement,
  American business, consumers, and farmers.
• Allowed more effective competition in the marketplace.

Congress of Industrial Organizations (1935): Founded within the American Federation of Labor (AFL), it was reorganized in 1938 by **John L. Lewis,** president of the United Mine Workers.
- Included other labor leaders expelled from the AFL.
- Had as its objective the industry-wide organizing of workers.
- Gained its first major victory when, after a 44-day sit-down strike in Flint, Michigan, General Motors recognized the **United Automobile Workers.**
- Achieved a second major success in 1937 when the Steel Workers Organizing Committee was recognized by U.S. Steel.

The "black cabinet": Term referring to blacks whom Roosevelt appointed to significant second-level positions.
- These officeholders included **Robert Weaver, William Haste,** and **Mary McLeod Bethune.**
- They consulted with each other and served as an active lobby for black interests.

Blacks: Reaped limited benefits from the New Deal.
- Civilian Conservation Corps had separate black camps.
- National Recovery Administration (NRA) codes tolerated unequal pay for blacks.
- Discriminatory practices in hiring and pay existed in relief agencies and in work relief programs.
- The first federally funded housing projects were segregated.
- The limited recognition blacks did receive contributed to their switch to the Democratic Party, a significant political alliance that would continue for decades.

Women: Made some gains under the New Deal.
- More than 100 women were named to federal government positions.
- Secretary of Labor **Frances Perkins** became the first female cabinet member.
- **Eleanor Roosevelt,** the First Lady and an advocate of women's rights, presided over an active network of women in the government.
- **Mary Dewson,** head of the **Women's Division of the Democratic National Committee,** increased women's role in the Democratic Party and helped secure federal appointments for women.
- The **Women's and Professional Projects Division** of the Work Progress Administration, under **Ellen Sullivan,** created programs that put women to work.
- On the negative side, New Deal programs were not especially supportive, relief agencies offered little employment, sexually

discriminating wage practices were sanctioned by the NRA, and domestic servants and waitresses were not covered by Social Security.

Native Americans: Benefited to some extent from the New Deal.
- The New Deal promoted an appreciation of the culture of Native Americans.
- **John Collier,** commissioner of the **Bureau of Indian Affairs,** promoted the **Indian Reorganization Act (1934).**
  1. Returned political authority to the tribes and gave them the right to own land collectively.
  2. Furnished government funds for education, health care, and cultural activities.

Theme 10 DEPRESSION, DIPLOMACY, AND WORLD WAR II

*T*he United States and the rest of the world suffered economically during the 1930s, and this worldwide depression produced political chaos. American isolationism turned to intervention after the Japanese attack on Pearl Harbor on December 7, 1941. The United States emerged from the war as a superpower and accepted a leading role in world diplomacy.

Key 55 American foreign policy in the 1930s

OVERVIEW *Franklin D. Roosevelt sought to improve the U.S. position in world trade and cultivated better relations with our American neighbors.*

Recognition of the Soviet Union (1933): Trade opportunities precipitated this event.
- In return for U.S. recognition, the Soviet Union promised not to interfere in U.S. domestic affairs.
- It also extended protection to U.S. citizens in the U.S.S.R.

Reciprocal Trade Agreement (1934): The president could raise or lower tariffs without congressional approval in return for reciprocal concessions from other nations. The volume of trade with other Western Hemisphere nations rose 100 percent during the decade.

Good neighbor policy: Developed by Secretary of State **Cordell Hull** at the **Seventh International Conference of American States,** held in Montevideo, Uruguay.
- The policy involved economic rather than political intervention, as begun under President Hoover.
- While the United States renounced unilateral intervention, it reserved the right to move against "outlaw" regimes. This policy represented a new American use of the Monroe Doctrine as a multilateral instrument for providing a buffer against threats from Europe.
- Examples included:
  1. Withdrawal of American marines from several Latin American nations.
  2. Congressional repeal, in 1934, of the **Platt Amendment,** which allowed U.S. intervention in Cuban affairs. The U.S. Navy still retained its base at Guantanamo Bay.

Buenos Aires Conference (1936): Roosevelt attended this conference, where the American states agreed to consult together whenever any one of them was threatened by aggression and to remain neutral if hostilities broke out between any two of them.

Declaration of Lima (1938): A commitment by the 21 American states that they would resist all threats to their peace and security.

Declaration of Panama (1939): Established a security zone around the Americas and warned belligerent powers not to undertake hostile action in the area.

Act of Havana (1940): A pledge by the foreign ministers of American states to prevent the transfer of any European possessions in the Western Hemisphere to any other European power.

Pittman Resolution (1940): Approved military and economic aid to any Latin American nations threatened by aggression; aim was to fortify Western Hemispheric defenses.

United States—Mexico Oil Agreement (1941): Prevented the nationalizing of American and British owned oil lands by the Mexican government of **Lazaro Cardenas.**
- The Mexican president had been moving the country toward socialism by nationalizing fertile land owned by foreigners for farmers, and by organizing labor into one union.
- A reciprocal agreement called for Mexico to pay for outstanding claims. Oil companies received $24 million in compensation for above-ground equipment.
- The United States provided humanitarian aid and trade agreements.

KEY QUOTATION

No state has the right to intervene in the internal or external affairs of another.

Montevideo Conference (1933)
Approved by 21 American states

Key 56 Preparation for war

OVERVIEW *Although isolationist feeling was strong and neutrality legislation supported such sentiments, by 1939 Roosevelt had slowly and skillfully turned America toward an internationalist approach. After Japan's attack on Pearl Harbor, the United States finally entered World War II.*

Nye munitions investigation (1934): A Senate committee under Senator **Gerald P. Nye** examined the influence of economic interests on America's decision to enter World War I.
- Concluded that profiteers, "merchants of death," maneuvered the United States into the war to save their investments.
- Resulted in isolationist sentiment and laws regulating foreign arms and munitions sales.

Neutrality Act (1935): Authorized the president to declare an embargo of up to 6 months on arms shipments to any country where a state of war existed.
- Also, he could forbid U.S. citizens from traveling on vessels of such countries except at their own risk.
- The act did not prohibit the sale of steel, copper, or oil.

Neutrality Act (1936): Continued the Neutrality Act of 1935 and added loans and credits to the list of items forbidden to belligerent nations.

Neutrality Act (1937): Authorized the president to determine when a state of war existed or a civil war was a threat to peace.
- In such cases he could place an embargo on the export of arms, ammunition, and credit.
- Belligerents could purchase only nonmilitary goods from the United States and must pay cash and ship their purchases themselves (i.e., **"cash and carry"**).

Neutrality Act (1939): Repealed the arms embargo for England and France.
- However, the cash-and-carry provision on all sales of munitions to belligerents was retained.
- The president could prohibit American ships from entering war zones.

Spanish Civil War (1936–37): The Falangists, under General **Francesco Franco,** revolted against the existing constitutional monarchy.

- They received aid from both Hitler and Mussolini against the Loyalists, who ultimately lost.
- Although the United States, France, and Britain offered no assistance to either side, American volunteers, the **Abraham Lincoln Brigade,** assisted the Loyalists.

"Quarantine" speech (October 5, 1937): Roosevelt indicated his opposition to the isolationist attitude of the neutrality acts.

- He recommended a "quarantine" of aggressors to preserve peace.
- The speech was also a response to Japan's aggression against China.

Panay incident (December 12, 1937): Japanese planes bombed the U.S. gunboat *Panay* and three oil tankers on the Yangtze River in China, killing two Americans. Yielding to American public pressure on the administration, the Japanese agreed to apologize for this "accident."

Selective Service and Training Act (Burke-Wadworth Act) (1940): Established the first peacetime military draft in America, and required the registration of men between 21 and 35 (later between 18 and 64).

National Defense Advisory Commission (May 1940): Headed by General Motors President **William B. Knudsen,** this agency was created to obtain materials, manage labor problems, control prices, supervise transportation, and encourage industrial and farm production. In January 1941, it became part of the **Office of Production Management.**

National Defense Research Committee (June 1940): Created to develop scientific research for military purposes.

- Worked with military departments, industry, and science.
- Was replaced by the **Office of Scientific Research and Development** in 1941.

Aid to Britain (September 1940): Two measures were significant:

- Roosevelt traded 50 U.S. World War I destroyers for 99-year leases on a number of British air and naval bases in the West Indies and the Atlantic.
- The **Lend-Lease Act (March 1941)** authorized the president to lend or lease arms and equipment to nations whose defense he considered vital to the United States. The act was designed to help Great Britain, but its provisions were extended to the U.S.S.R. in 1941.

War preparation viewpoints: Two opposing groups sought to influence Congress and the public.
- **Committee to Defend America by Aiding the Allies:** Led by journalist **William Allen White,** it advocated intervention in World War II.
- **America First Committee:** Established by **Charles Lindbergh,** Senator **Gerald Nye,** and former NRA head **Hugh Johnson,** it agitated to keep America out of the war.

Atlantic Charter (1941): Document issued by Roosevelt and Churchill during their secret meeting near Newfoundland; it proclaimed war aims and common principles.

The four freedoms (1941): Cited by Roosevelt in a speech to Congress, the four freedoms consisted of freedom of speech, freedom of religion, freedom from want, and freedom from fear.

Undeclared naval war (1941): Four events were significant:
- In September, a German U-boat fired on the American destroyer *Greer.*
- Roosevelt ordered American ships to fire on German submarines "on sight."
- When the *Reuben James,* an American destroyer, was sunk by Nazi submarines in October, American sailors died.
- Congress then ratified a bill allowing merchant vessels to be armed and to sail into belligerent ports.

Pearl Harbor (December 7, 1941): Japanese assets in the United States had been frozen in response to Japanese aggression in Asia.
- While negotiations trying to reverse this action were under way, the Japanese attacked Pearl Harbor, killing over 2,000 Americans.
- On December 8 the United States declared war against Japan, and on December 11, against Italy and Germany.

Key 57 Organizing the war effort

OVERVIEW *Although some preparations had taken place before America declared war against the Axis powers, the actual shift from civilian to war production began thereafter, producing major changes in American society.*

Election of 1940: Roosevelt won 55 percent of the popular vote and a third term in office.
- The Republican candidate, businessman **Wendell Willkie,** promised to keep the nation out of war while assisting the Allies.
- This position was echoed by Roosevelt.
- Willkie attempted to use the three-term issue to arouse public fears but was unsuccessful.

War Powers Act (December 1941): Gave the president emergency authority to create new executive agencies and reorganize existing ones.
- Established control over trade.
- Initiated defense contracts.
- Provided for censorship.

War Powers Act (March 1942): Enabled the president to requisition property, enforce priorities, establish ration controls, and regulate transportation services.

Office of Price Administration (January 1942): Set price ceilings on all goods except farm produce, and established rent controls to protect consumers' interests and prevent inflation.

War Production Board (January 1942): Supervised production and supply.
- Authorized to obtain raw materials and allot them to certain industries.
- Made contracts.
- Regulated production and eliminated nonessential civilian production.

National War Labor Board (January 1942): Mediated labor disputes to prevent strikes in war industries; was later given authority to stabilize wages.

War Manpower Commission (April 1942): Created to determine how industry, agriculture, and government could be ensured of adequate labor supply.

Office of War Information (June 1942): Coordinated war news issued by government agencies, and used press, motion pictures, and radio to convey this information to Americans.

Office of Strategic Services (June 1942): Created to engage in intelligence activities in foreign countries and to evaluate intelligence information.

Office of Civilian Defense (1942): Directed a program of civilian defense in case of a direct attack on the United States. Plans were made for air raid precautions, first aid instruction, and fire protection.

"No strike" pledge and "little steel" formula: During the war, unions agreed not to stop production by striking. The National War Labor Board negotiated the little steel formula, which set a 15 percent limit on wage increases.

Anti-inflation Act (1942): Authorized the administration to freeze agricultural prices, salaries, wages, and rents.
- Created the Office of Economic Stabilization.
- Controlled all economic phases of the war effort.
- Aimed to stabilize the economy and hold down war costs.

Revenue Act (1942): Increased corporate income taxes to a maximum of 40 percent and set a flat rate of 90 percent on excess profits.
- Required more people to file tax returns.
- Initiated a system of payroll deductions and tax withholding to take effect by 1943.

Smith-Connally Act (1943): Enabled the president to seize plants where war production was threatened by strikes.
- Forbade agitation in plants seized by the government.
- Required 30 days' notice before a strike could be called, with unions held liable if such notice was not given.

Key 58 Minorities and women
during the war

OVERVIEW *The war served to improve the conditions for some minorities and women, yet it also proved to be a time of prejudice and discrimination for others.*

Blacks and industry: In 1941, **A. Philip Randolph,** president of the **Brotherhood of Sleeping Car Porters,** demanded that the government require companies receiving defense contracts to integrate their work forces. His planned march on Washington was cancelled in return for the creation of a **Fair Employment Practices Commission,** which would investigate discrimination against blacks in war industries.

Other changes involving blacks: Included were the following:
* Black migration increased dramatically from the rural South to industrial cities in the North.
* Riots involving blacks occurred throughout the war in 41 cities.
* The **Congress of Racial Equality (CORE)** was established in 1942 and implemented aggressive tactics, such as sit-ins and demonstrations against segregation.
* In *Smith* v. *Allwright* **(1944),** the Supreme Court ruled that Texas's all-white primary election was unconstitutional.
* Several training camps and bases were partially integrated in the armed services.

Mexican-Americans: In 1942, the Mexican and American governments agreed to a program by which Mexican contract laborers would be admitted to the United States to work for a limited time.
* The labor shortage provided these laborers with opportunities to work in factories instead of only on farms.
* The presence of teenagers, some of whom belonged to street gangs, created conflicts in Anglo communities.
* In June 1943, riots against these Mexican-American "zoot suiters" (so called because of their style of dress), in response to their alleged attacks on servicemen, resulted in a Los Angeles law prohibiting the wearing of the suits.

Native Americans: During the war, many Indians served in military communications.
* Many left reservations to work in war production.

- The wartime atmosphere encouraged conformity and undermined the revitalization of tribal autonomy.

Japanese internment: The war produced racial animosity toward Japanese and Japanese-Americans.
- **Nisei** were American citizens of Japanese ancestry, **Issei,** unnaturalized Japanese-born immigrants living in the United States.
- West Coast residents demanded protection against alleged Japanese spies.
- Roosevelt approved a War Department plan to intern Japanese-Americans in relocation camps, in the interest of national security, until the war's end.
  1. The **War Relocation Authority** carried out the policy.
  2. Families were given a few days to dispose of their belongings and prepare for relocation.
  3. First they were sent to temporary assembly centers, then to one of ten permanent camps in California, Arizona, Utah, Colorado, Wyoming, Idaho, and Arkansas.
  4. Relocation camps had barbed wire perimeters, and residents lived communally.
  5. In 1944 the Supreme Court upheld the constitutionality of the relocations *(Korematsu* v. *United States),* but later that year, after Roosevelt's reelection, most Japanese-Americans were released.
- Relocation centers for German-Americans and Italian-Americans also existed for a time, though never to the extent of Japanese centers.

Women during the war: Women played an active role in the war effort.
- Women's branches of the armed services (e.g., WAVES, WACS) were created.
- The number of women in the workforce increased by about 60 percent, with women taking jobs vacated by servicemen.
- Most new workers were married and were older.
- Most worked in heavy industrial jobs (e.g., as riveters, welders, blast furnace cleaners, drill press operators), giving rise to the name **"Rosie the riveter."**
- Women were faced with pay inequities, scarce child-care facilities, and even inequitable treatment as union members.
- After the war, women were forced to leave their temporary positions and return to full-time roles as housewives and mothers so that veterans could have their jobs back.

Key 59 The war's end

OVERVIEW *By 1943, America and its allies had stopped the advance of the Axis powers. They then took the offensive, which ultimately led to the defeat of Germany and Japan. Wartime diplomacy seemed to forecast the Cold War that followed. President Roosevelt's death from a stroke on April 12, 1945, resulted in a change of leadership, escalating suspicions between the superpowers.*

Casablanca Conference (January 1943): Roosevelt and Churchill agreed to establish a second front in Europe, to invade Europe through Sicily and Italy, and to continue the war until the "unconditional surrender" of all enemies.

Teheran Conference (November–December 1943): Roosevelt, Stalin, and Churchill agreed to open a second front within 6 months.
- Russia pledged to enter the war against Japan when Germany was defeated.
- An international organization for peace was planned.

Dumbarton Oaks Conference (1944): Representatives of the United States, Great Britain, the U.S.S.R., and China formulated a plan to create the **United Nations (UN).**
- Every nation would be represented in the General Assembly.
- Five permanent members (the United States, Britain, France, the U.S.S.R., and China) would constitute the Security Council, along with temporary delegates from other nations.
- Each major power could veto Security Council decisions.
- These agreements were the basis for the drafting of the UN charter at a conference of 50 nations in San Francisco, during April 1945.
- The UN charter was ratified on August 8, 1945, by the U.S. Senate.

Election of 1944: Running against Roosevelt was 42-year-old **Thomas E. Dewey,** Republican governor of New York.
- He received strong support from labor's CIO **Political Action Committee,** an organization led by **Sidney Hillman** and **Philip Murray.**
- The Democrats supported Roosevelt's administration and promised to begin postwar planning.

- The Republicans criticized waste and inefficiency, but supported Roosevelt's foreign policy.
- Roosevelt received 53 percent of the popular vote.

GI Bill of Rights (1944): Provided education, medical care, job training, unemployment pensions, and compensation, and offered mortgage loans to male and female war veterans.

Yalta Conference (February 1945): Roosevelt, Churchill, and Stalin agreed to divide a defeated Germany into occupation zones.
- Also the U.S.S.R. was given half of Poland and other territory in the Far East, including an occupation zone in Korea and possession of the Kurile and Sakhalin islands.
- The plan for the United Nations was also ratified.

Victory in Europe Day (V-E Day): When Germany surrendered to the Allies on May 8, 1945, the war in Europe ended.

Potsdam Conference (July 1945): Truman, Attlee, and Stalin drew up plans for the reconstruction of Europe and for dealing with a defeated Germany.
- The Council of Foreign Ministers was created to draw up peace treaties for the Axis powers.
- The **Potsdam Declaration** (July 26, 1945) demanded Japan's unconditional surrender.

Hiroshima (August 6, 1945) and Nagasaki (August 9, 1945): The United States dropped an atomic bomb, secretly developed during the war via the Manhattan Project, on these two Japanese cities, and the Japanese surrendered soon afterward.

Victory over Japan Day (V-J Day): On August 15, 1945, the war with Japan ended. On September 2, 1945, surrender papers were signed on the deck of the battleship *Missouri.*

War crimes trials: An international military tribunal tried major war criminals at Nuremberg, Germany (1945-46) and in Tokyo, Japan (1946–48). In Germany, 12 criminals were sentenced to be hanged; in Japan, 7.

Key 60 Legacy of World War II

OVERVIEW *The war had a major impact on America's domestic and foreign policies and shaped the events of the postwar period.*

New U.S. position: The United States emerged with minor casualties compared to the other Allies and to the Axis powers.
- It was the only nation possessing the atomic bomb.
- It became a superpower and assumed leadership in world affairs.

Economy: The war had a profound effect on the U.S. economy.
- Many items were rationed during the war and continued to be in short supply for some time thereafter.
- After Roosevelt's death, some wanted to dismantle the "welfare state."
- Others wanted to continue the progress made in regard to the unemployed, the elderly, health care, and race relations.
- People feared a return of economic depression after the war.

Legacy: Federal bureaucracy expanded dramatically during the war, as did federal power.
- Government became the single most important force in American life.
- Geographic mobility increased as labor shortages created job opportunities.
- Blacks, women, and Mexican-Americans benefited.
- Pent up consumer demands exploded after the war.
- Higher birthrate accompanied an increase in marriages for returning veterans, foreshadowing the "baby boom"; war separation also led to an increased divorce rate for some.

Theme 11 POLITICS AND THE
COLD WAR

*T*ensions latent between the United States and the U.S.S.R. during World War II surfaced at the end of the hostilities. This strained relationship, characterized as the "Cold War," produced hostility and suspicion between the two superpowers and deeply affected American foreign and domestic policy. An outbreak of antiradical hysteria surfaced as the United States reconverted to a peacetime economy.

INDIVIDUAL KEYS IN THIS THEME

Key 61 Truman administration:
Foreign policy

OVERVIEW *After Franklin D. Roosevelt's untimely death in April 1945, Harry S Truman assumed the presidency. Largely inexperienced in foreign policy, he viewed the Soviet Union with suspicion and dislike.*

Containment: George F. Kennan, an influential diplomat, proclaimed that U.S. policy toward the Soviet Union should focus on the containment of Russia's expansive tendencies, a principle later enunciated as the Truman Doctrine.

Truman Doctrine: President Truman's foreign policy principle, stated before Congress on March 12, 1947.
- It viewed communism as an ideological threat that must be met anywhere in the world, even if it did not directly involve the Soviet Union.
- It urged American economic and military aid to any nation threatened by communism.
- In accord with the doctrine, Congress approved $400 million in aid to Greece and Turkey to fight Communist aggression.

Marshall Plan: Announced by Secretary of State **George C. Marshall** at a Harvard University commencement in 1947.
- Approved by Congress in 1948 and known as the **European Recovery Program,** it granted over $12 billion of economic assistance to European nations.
- The Soviet Union and its eastern satellites rejected this assistance.
- The plan's purpose was both humanitarian and political.
- An economically prosperous Europe would aid America's growth and would also impede the advance of communism.
- The **Mutual Security Act (1951)** continued the foreign aid program (both military and economic) started under the Marshall Plan.

Atomic Energy Commission (1946): Established by the **McMahon Act,** it promoted the use of atomic energy for peaceful purposes and safeguarded national security.

National Security Act (1947): Established a new **Department of Defense,** the **National Security Council (NSC),** and the **Central Intelligence Agency (CIA).**
- The NSC supervised foreign and military policy through the president, several cabinet members, and other advisers.
- The CIA was responsible for collecting information through open and covert methods and for engaging in secret political and military operations abroad.
- Through this act the executive branch expanded its control over all defense activities.

Rio Treaty (1947): The United States and 20 other American nations agreed to provide for the security of all American nations against acts of aggression. All would determine what action to take against an aggressor of any one of them.

Berlin airlift (1948–49): England, France, and the United States had merged their occupation zones into a new West German republic.
- The U.S.S.R. then prohibited all land traffic between Berlin and West Germany.
- In response, the American Air Force air lifted needed supplies to West Berlin for almost a year until Stalin lifted the blockade.
- In October 1949, Germany was officially divided.

North Atlantic Treaty Organization (NATO) (1949): Formed by 12 Western European nations, declaring that an armed attack against one member constituted an attack against all. NATO countries would maintain a military force in Europe as defense against a possible Soviet invasion.

Warsaw Pact (1955): A response to NATO, this military alliance aligned the Soviet Union with Poland, East Germany, Hungary, Czechoslovakia, Romania, and Bulgaria.

Soviets explode atomic bomb (1949): This shocking revelation by President Truman on September 22, 1949, encouraged the arms races between the superpowers.

Point Four Program (1949): Proposed by President Truman, it offered technical assistance, sponsored and financed largely by the United States, to underdeveloped nations.
- Approved by Congress, it encouraged foreign trade.
- It also helped to halt Communist expansion around the world.

Establishment of Communist China (1949): The Nationalist forces under **Chiang Kai-shek** were defeated by the Communist forces and fled to the island of Taiwan in December 1949. The United States did not recognize the Maoist government as the legitimate Chinese government.

Japan as ally: American occupation of Japan ended in 1951, when a peace treaty was signed. A security treaty, also signed, gave the United States military bases in Japan.

Conflict in Korea: In 1948, the Republic of (South) Korea was established, as well as the People's Republic (North Korea).
- In 1949, the U.S.S.R. and the United States withdrew their military forces from North and South Korea, respectively.
- On June 25, 1950, North Korean troops, alleging an attack, entered South Korea.
- The UN Security Council ordered North Korea to withdraw.
- UN and U.S. troops fought in this "police action," which was actually a limited war.
- When **Douglas MacArthur,** commander of the troops, sought to expand military operations against the Chinese, he was removed from his command by President Truman.
- Under General **Matthew Ridgway,** armistice negotiations began in 1951, and in 1953 North Korea and the United Nations reached an armistice agreement.
- A cease-fire line, north of the **38th parallel,** was established.
- In 1954 the United States and South Korea signed a treaty guaranteeing U.S. assistance if South Korea was attacked.

United States-Philippines Security Treaty (1951): The two nations agreed to consult together on measures of self-defense in case of an armed attack on either.

ANZUS Treaty (1951): The United States, Australia, and New Zealand agreed to settle disputes among themselves peacefully and to consult together when any signer was threatened by an attack in the Pacific area. A council of foreign ministers was established to carry out the treaty.

Key 62 Truman administration:
Domestic policy

OVERVIEW *The postwar years brought both prosperity and economic problems to the United States. The federal government's increased expenditures for defense and domestic programs were partly responsible for the nation's prosperity. Inflation and labor strife created economic unrest.*

General economic picture: Marked by several trends:
- The rise in the birthrate increased the demand for goods and services, which in turn encouraged consumer spending.
- A growth in business and government bureaucracy and greater diversification of corporations occurred.
- White collar and service employment rose, and women's participation in the labor force increased.
- Agriculture declined as an occupation.
- More people flocked to urban centers and suburbs.

Reconversion: Economic problems resulted with the transition from a wartime to a peacetime economy.
- The **Civilian Productions Administration,** created in 1945, promoted the reconversion from wartime to civilian production.
- In less than a year the armed forces were reduced from 12 million to 3 million.
- The sudden outpouring of consumer demand produced runaway inflation.

Labor strikes: Economic difficulties caused major strikes in the automobile, electrical, railroad, mining, and steel industries.
- In 1946, for example, 400,000 United Mine Workers went on strike.
- After coal fields had been shut down for 40 days, the government seized the mines.

Fair Deal: Term used to describe President Truman's new liberal agenda, which consisted of a 21-point domestic program submitted to Congress on September 16, 1945.
- In the New Deal tradition, it advocated expanding Social Security benefits, increasing the minimum wage, a full employment

program, slum clearance, public housing, and government sponsorship of scientific research.
- Other proposals were added later, but congressional conservatism blocked these reforms.

Employment Act (1946): Supported the use of government spending to spur economic growth and established a **Council of Economic Advisors,** appointed by the president and responsible to him.

Fulbright Act (1946): Provided scholarships for U.S. students to study in foreign countries. Funds came from payments made by foreign countries in their own currency after purchasing U.S. surplus equipment.

Legislative Reorganization Act (1946): Streamlined many Congressional procedures.
- Reduced standing committees.
- Increased congressional salaries to $12,500.

President's Committee on Civil Rights (1946): Issued a report entitled "To Secure These Rights," which advocated stronger civil rights laws.
- While no civil rights legislation was passed, Truman began the desegregation of the armed forces,.
- He also appointed black judges to federal courts and issued an executive order barring discrimination in federal employment.

Presidential Succession Act (1947): Spelled out the succession to the presidency after the vice president: Speaker of the House of Representatives, president pro tempore of the Senate, secretary of state, and other cabinet members.

Taft-Hartley Act (1947): Known as the **Labor-Management Relations Act** and considered antiunion, it was vetoed by Truman but approved by a congressional override.
- Prohibited the closed shop.
- Required union leaders to take a non-Communist oath.
- Forbade union contributions to political campaigns.
- Required unions to have public financial statements.
- Established a 60-day cooling-off period before striking.
- Allowed suits against unions for broken contracts and damages.
- Symbolized the end of New Deal reform, effected by the Republican-controlled 80th Congress.

Public Housing Administration (1947): Created slum clearance projects and low-rent and emergency housing projects, and also managed and disposed of emergency housing and similar projects instituted during the war.

Election of 1948: Often cited as an example of polling inaccuracy.
- The Democratic convention was split.
    1. Southern conservatives formed the States' Rights ("Dixiecrat") Party and nominated South Carolina Governor **Strom Thurmond** for president. The party opposed the civil rights plank in the Democratic platform.
    2. Liberals formed a new Progressive Party and ran **Henry A. Wallace** for president. The party favored gradual socialism, the abolition of racial segregation, and a conciliatory attitude toward Russia.
- Governor **Thomas E. Dewey** of New York was the Republican's choice; his views were not substantially different from Truman's.
- Calling a special session of a "do-nothing" Republican Congress, Truman failed to get them to enact their platform's liberal measures.
- Truman supported civil rights, increased price supports for farmers, and repeal of the Taft-Hartley Act.
- He won a narrow victory, 49.5 percent of the popular vote, although polls had predicted a victory for Dewey.

Fair Deal legislation: After the election, the 81st Congress was not cooperative as Truman attempted to win approval for civil rights legislation, health insurance, and aid to education. On the positive side:
- Congress extended some New Deal reforms by increasing the minimum wage and expanding Social Security by raising benefits and extending coverage to more Americans.
- The **National Housing Act (1949)** authorized the construction of low-income housing units over 6 years, accompanied by long-term rent subsidies.

Key 63 The Cold War at home

OVERVIEW *Postwar America was characterized by a fear of Communist subversion.*

House Un-American Activities Committee (HUAC): Established under Franklin D. Roosevelt in 1938, it was designed to disclose foreign influences in the United States.
- In 1947, Republicans launched investigations to link Democratic rule with Communist subversion.
- The HUAC investigated the film industry, charging that American films contained Soviet propaganda.

Alien Registration Act (Smith Act) (1940): Set criminal penalties for teaching or advocating revolution, or for belonging to a group that did either.
- It required aliens to register with federal authorities.
- Under it, 11 Communist leaders were convicted in 1949 of conspiring to teach the violent overthrow of the U.S. government.
- Forty other Communist leaders were convicted and imprisoned in 1951 for violating the act.

Federal Loyalty Program (1947): Designed to review the "loyalty" of federal employees.
- "Loyalty boards" investigated federal workers, and in 1950 Truman authorized the dismissal, in sensitive departments, of those labeled as bad security risks.
- By 1951, 212 employees had been dismissed and over 2,000 had resigned.
- State and local governments then launched similar programs, while courts handed down harsh sentences to defendants accused of subversion.
- Colleges, schools, and unions also began to root out Communist sympathizers.

Alger Hiss: A former State Department official against whom charges were leveled by **Whittaker Chambers,** a confessed Soviet agent.
- Accusing Hiss of stealing State Department documents, Chambers led investigators to Hiss's farm, where microfilm copies of documents were found in a hollowed-out pumpkin.
- After two trials, Hiss was convicted of perjury (lying to the HUAC) and was sentenced to 5 years in prison.

McCarran Internal Security Act (1950): Enacted over Truman's veto, it required all Communist organizations to register with the government and to publish their records.

- Communists were denied passports and were prohibited from working in defense plants.
- Individuals affiliated with "subversive organizations" overseas were denied U.S. visas.

Civil Defense Act (1951): Created the **Federal Civil Defense Administration,** which would develop a plan of defense against atomic attack, and assisted local and state civil defense agencies to enact their programs.

Ethel and Julius Rosenberg: Convicted of atomic espionage and sentenced to death in 1951.

- Public protests and appeals to the Supreme Court failed.
- The death sentences were carried out in 1953.

McCarran-Walter Act (1952): Passed over Truman's veto.

- Codified all existing restrictions on immigration.
- Retained the quota system, but removed discrimination against Asians.
- Gave the attorney-general the right to deport certain undesirables.

Joseph McCarthy: As Republican Senator from Wisconsin (1947–57), he became the leading crusader against communism.

- During a speech in 1950, in Wheeling, West Virginia, he claimed to possess a list of 205 known Communists currently employed in the State Department.
- He attacked the Truman and Eisenhower administrations for allowing communists to hold government positions.
- In his highly publicized investigation of subversion, which examined various branches of the government, he did not produce conclusive evidence that any federal employees had Communist ties.
- On December 2, 1954, the Senate voted to censure him.

Election of 1952: Illinois Governor **Adlai E. Stevenson,** the Democratic candidate, favored by liberals and intellectuals, was defeated by the Republican candidate, General **Dwight D. Eisenhower,** a war hero and former commander of NATO.

- The Republicans promised to end the Korean War and accused the Democrats of being soft on communism and of tolerating corruption in Washington.
- Eisenhower received 55 percent of the popular vote.

Theme 12 THE AGE OF
AMERICAN AFFLUENCE

*A*fter 1945, abundance and affluence were dominant aspects of American society. But not everyone shared in this prosperity and optimism. While the U.S. middle class enjoyed rising living standards, many other Americans, particularly blacks, lived in poverty.

Key 64 The postindustrial society

OVERVIEW *Compared to the situation in the 1920s, American economic growth after 1945 was more widely distributed and better balanced. Technological changes and steady economic growth, fueled by government and military spending, were characteristic trends. Unemployment remained around 5 percent, and inflation hovered about 3 percent.*

Keynesian economic theory: Became widely adopted by economists and the public during the 1950s.
- It fostered a belief in permanent economic stability and growth.
- Keynes asserted that, by varying the flow of government spending and managing the currency supply, the government could stimulate the economy, cure recession, and curb growth to prevent inflation.

Consolidation: A trend in both business and farming.
- Over 4,000 corporate mergers occurred in the 1950s, and corporations changed from being single-industry firms to diversified conglomerates.
- Agricultural consolidation also took place, and **agribusiness** emerged, when much of the productive farmland was purchased by corporations and financial institutions.

Labor and unions: Union membership remained stable in the 1950s, and many unions became powerful and affluent bureaucracies.
- In 1955, under **George Meany,** the American Federation of Labor and the Congress of Industrial Organizations became the **AFL-CIO.**
- The **Teamsters** and the **United Mine Workers** were plagued by scandals of corruption and violence.

Consumer culture: Prosperity produced a middle-class consumer culture, fostered by advertising, increased variety and availability of products, along with the existence of credit cards, revolving charge accounts, and easy-payment plans.

Growth of suburbs: During the 1950s, one-third of the U.S. population settled in suburbs.
- Mass-production techniques in housing construction, such as those pioneered in **Levittown,** New York, along with increased affluence, encouraged suburbanization.

- Suburban families found privacy, security, space (for consumer goods) in larger homes, and a sense of community.
- Suburbs were similar in that they were mostly white and had a class component.

Baby and Child Care: A famous, widely used child-centered guide to child rearing, by **Dr. Benjamin Spock.**
- Reflected the decade's emphasis on family life.
- Featured the middle-class woman in her role as a mother.
- Encouraged women to stay at home.

Television: Replaced radio and movies as the main source of entertainment in the 1950s.
- Shaped American culture and served to homogenize American language and life.
- Conveyed news and entertainment, while introducing viewers to new products and fashions.
- Evoked powerlessness, alienation, and other emotions in its audience and thus could act as a force for social change or traditional values.

Science and technology: The hallmarks of the decade.
- Reverence, pride, and fascination were typical public reactions to the jet plane, computer, and U.S. space program.
- After the Soviet Union's launching of a satellite, called **Sputnik,** science education, research, and the American space program (established in 1958) received increased funding and support.

Bureaucracies: Were highly influential in the lives of both blue- and white-collar Americans during the 1950s.
- Educational institutions responded by training specialists in a wide variety of fields in the "multiversity."
- Bureaucracies symbolized the impersonalized nature of modern society and became the subject of books such as **Willliam H. Whyte's** *The Organization Man.*

Outgroups: Persons (e.g., farmers, blacks, Hispanics, rural whites) who did not share in the affluence of the 1950s.
- Farmers experienced a decline in their incomes along with price increases in consumer goods.
- Black, Puerto Rican, and Mexican ghettos expanded.
- These urban "prisoners," like the rural poor, lacked adequate schools, health care, and other services.

Key 65 Origins of the civil rights
movement

OVERVIEW *The germination of the civil rights movement
occurred during the 1950s as the Supreme Court issued its
desegregation decision. The Cold War indicated the need to
confront racial injustice at home. In addition, urban communities of blacks began organizing, pressuring, and
protesting, thus making their cause highly visible to the rest
of the United States.*

***Brown* v. *Board of Education of Topeka, Kansas* (1954):** In a unani-
mous decision by the Supreme Court, the segregation of blacks and
whites in public schools was declared unconstitutional.
- The decision reversed the 1896 "separate but equal" ruling of
  Plessy* v. *Ferguson.
- It directed local school authorities to implement desegregation
  "with all deliberate speed."
- State and local governments, particularly in the South, often
  defied or delayed this directive.

Little Rock segregation issue (September 1957): When Central High
School in Little Rock, Arkansas, was directed to admit nine black students, Governor **Orval Faubus** used the National Guard to prevent
their admission.
- Under court order Faubus removed the National Guard.
- The black students entered school but were removed by local
  authorities for fear of mob violence.
- President Eisenhower then sent federal troops, which were withdrawn in November, to enforce the court order.

Rosa Parks: Arrested on December 1, 1955, in Montgomery, Alabama,
for refusing to give up her seat on a bus to a white passenger.
- In response, the city's black community organized a successful
  boycott of the bus system to force an end to such segregation.
- The boycott ended after the Supreme Court ruled that racial segregation in public transit systems is unconstitutional.

Dr. Martin Luther King, Jr.: Secured recognition in the civil rights
movement by leading the Montgomery bus boycott.

- He was a local Baptist pastor, new to the area, whose father was a leading Atlanta minister.
- He advocated passive, nonviolent resistance as a means of protesting and encouraged blacks to employ such methods.
- As head of the interracial **Southern Christian Leadership Conference,** he became the most influential and most admired American black leader.
- He was assassinated in 1968, and during the 1980s his birthday became a national holiday.

Eisenhower's role in regard to civil rights: Completed the integration of the armed forces, tried to desegregate the federal work force, and signed a **Civil Rights Act** in 1957.

- Although a weak bill with few provisions for enforcement, it created a **Commission on Civil Rights** to investigate alleged violations of the right to vote, based on race, religion, color, or national origin.
- Intimidation or coercion to stop people from voting was prohibited.

Key 66 Eisenhower's domestic policy

OVERVIEW *Dwight D. Eisenhower, familiarly known as Ike, was a conservative and a behind-the-scenes president. His presidential style avoided confrontation and offered little leadership initiative. Although he was cautious and his policies were moderate, he did intensify the U.S. commitment to oppose communism. His was a business-oriented administration.*

Department of Health, Education, and Welfare (HEW): Created on April 1, 1953; the first secretary was **Oveta Culp Hobby.** The new department coordinated all the activities of the government's welfare agencies.

Other social programs fostered by Eisenhower: Included extending the Social Security system and unemployment compensation to more people, as well as increasing the hourly minimum wage to $1.00.

Small Business Administration: Established in 1953 to replace the **Reconstruction Finance Corporation,** it provided loans and other government aid to small businesses.

St. Lawrence Seaway Project: Approved under the **Seaway Act** (1954), it sponsored the construction of the St. Lawrence Seaway linking the Great Lakes with the Atlantic Ocean.

Housing Act (1955): Provided for the construction of 45,000 new public housing units per year for 4 years.

Soil Bank Act (1956): Authorized payments to farmers who kept acreage out of production under an acreage-reserve program, and who would devote acreage to trees, grass, or water storage under a conservation reserve program.

Federal Aid Highway Act (1956): Provided $26 billion over a 10-year period for building a national highway system. A highway "trust fund" raised money for the program through new taxes on fuel, tires, cars, and trucks.

Election of 1956: The Republican incumbent, Eisenhower, received almost 57 percent of the popular vote.
• Democrat **Adlai E. Stevenson** was again defeated.

- Election issues included the question of radioactive fallout from hydrogen bomb testing, the continuation of the draft, and civil rights.

National Defense Education Act (1958): Provided $300 million for loans to college students preparing to teach or possessing ability in science, mathematics, foreign languages, or engineering.
- Funds were also delegated to strengthen instruction in these areas.
- National defense fellowships were created, and $15 million was allocated annually to the states to identify and encourage able students.

Labor Reform Act (1959): Assured union members greater participation in union affairs via a "bill of rights," and provided for publicity of union affairs to end abuses and corruption.

Key 67 Foreign affairs under Eisenhower

OVERVIEW *In the Eisenhower years Truman's commitment to containment as a global effort to resist communist subversion was continued.*

Global concerns: Two factors joined to help develop policy.
- The threat of nuclear war between the superpowers, which caused the development of more weapons, sometimes in excess of the need, thus establishing what Eisenhower warned about: a **military-industrial complex.**
- The development of a consistent policy toward new Third World nations, balancing their need for setting national goals while helping them avoid control by local Communists or the Soviet Union.

John F. Dulles: As secretary of state under Eisenhower (1953–59), he was the architect of **"massive retaliation"** and **"brinkmanship."**
- Fiercely anti-Communist, he called for the **"liberation"** of Iron Curtain countries.
- He believed the United States should respond to Communist threats through *"massive retaliation,"* which meant using nuclear weapons.
- *"Brinksmanship"* meant going to the brink of war with the Soviet Union to keep peace and obtain concessions. Such a policy relied on nuclear weapons rather than on expensive conventional armed forces, thereby providing "more bang for the buck."
- Dulles's policy also included the creation of several **mutual defense pacts** based on NATO.

United States-South Korea Security Treaty (1953): The two nations agreed to act together in meeting an armed attack on either in the Pacific area. At Korea's request, U.S. forces would be stationed in and about Korea.

Baghdad Pact or CENTO Alliance (1953): Called the Central Treaty Organization, this mutual defense pact included the United States, Great Britain, Turkey, Pakistan, Iraq, and Iran.

Southeast Asia Treaty Organization (SEATO) (1954): Stipulated that all parties would initiate a self-help and mutual aid program

developing the capacity to resist armed attack and preventing subversive activities from outside.
- Designed to prevent Communist expansion in the Pacific.
- Included the United States, Great Britain, France, Australia, New Zealand, the Philippines, Thailand, and Pakistan.

Relations with China: Developments included:
- The **Formosa Resolution** (1955), approved by Congress, authorized the president to make use of armed forces, if needed, to protect Formosa and the Pescardores Islands.
- **United States-China Security Treaty,** agreed to in 1955, stated that Nationalist China and the United States would jointly resist both armed attack and Communist subversive activities directed against either nation.
  1. The treaty pertained to Formosa, the Pescardores Islands, and U.S. territories in the Western Pacific.
  2. Nationalist China granted the United States the right to station armed forces in Formosa.

Geneva Summit Conference (1955, 1957): A disarmament program based on Eisenhower's **"open skies" plan** was referred to the Conference of Foreign Ministers. Other issues discussed included German unification, exchange of ideas and goods, lowering travel barriers, and a plan for a U.S.-U.S.S.R. summit meeting.

Nuclear arms race: The **Atomic Energy Commission** developed and tested the hydrogen bomb during this decade. The first test took place in the South Pacific in 1954.
- The **distant early warning (DEW)** line of radar stations was installed in Canada and in Alaska in 1958.
- Also in 1958, an **intercontinental ballistic missile (ICBM)** was launched, and by 1960 nuclear submarines, carrying atomic-tipped missiles, had been developed.
- Nuclear testing in the atmosphere became a major concern.

The Central Intelligence Agency (CIA): Conducted several operations to change the form of foreign governments.
- In 1953 CIA agents overthrew Iran's premier.
- In 1954 the CIA supported a coup in Guatemala.
- The CIA was unsuccessful, however, in overthrowing Indonesia's leader in 1958 and Cuba's Fidel Castro in 1961.

Europe: The "Iron Curtain" solidified during the 1950s.
- In 1954 West Germany began to rearm; and by 1957 German forces had joined NATO and Germany had become a U.S. ally.

- A Hungarian nationalist revolt in 1956 was crushed by the U.S.S.R., which installed a pro-Soviet government.

Vietnam-Geneva Agreement (1954): Eisenhower had refused the French request for American military intervention in Vietnam. After the fall of Dien Bien Phu, France agreed to meet with **Ho Chi Minh,** leader of Vietnam's nationalist forces, in Geneva.
- The **Geneva Accords** (July 1954) temporarily divided Vietnam along the 17th parallel.
  1. The North was placed under Ho Chi Minh's control, while the South would be governed by a pro-Western regime.
  2. In 1956 democratic elections would unite the nation.
- The United States, fearing that a Communist government would result from elections, helped establish a pro-American government in the South under **Ngo Dinh Diem,** who would not allow the elections to take place.

Domino theory: This analogy held that, if Vietnam became Communist, the rest of Asia, like of row of dominoes, would also fall under Communist control.

Suez Canal crisis: In 1952 Egypt gained independence from Britain, and in 1954 **Gamal Abdel Nasser** assumed power.
- Soviet arms were exchanged for Egyptian cotton.
- The Soviets offered to finance a Nile River dam; the United States countered with a similar offer but withdrew it in 1956, as Nasser flirted with the U.S.S.R.
- Nasser nationalized the Suez Canal, run by an Anglo-French company.
- Israeli, British, and French forces invaded Egypt to take the canal by force.
- The United States joined the United Nations in condemning this action.
- The French and British withdrew, while Egypt and Israel agreed to a cease-fire. Thereafter, Egypt turned to the Soviet Union for assistance.

Eisenhower Doctrine (1957): Offered U.S. economic and military aid to ensure the territorial independence of Middle Eastern nations threatened by armed aggression from Communist countries.
- In 1957 the doctrine was invoked to assist **King Hussein** of Jordan.
- In 1958 marines were sent to aid Lebanon.

Cuba (1959): Fidel Castro established a new government in Cuba after overthrowing the **Batista** regime.

- In 1960 it accepted Soviet assistance.
- By 1961 the United States had severed diplomatic relations with Castro.
- Cuba developed an alliance with the Soviet Union.

U-2 spy plane incident: In 1959 **Nikita S. Khrushchev,** premier of the Soviet Union, visited the United States and conferred with Eisenhower at Camp David.
- However, Khrushchev cancelled a planned May 1960 summit meeting in Paris after Eisenhower admitted authorizing the flight of a U-2 spy plane shot down over Soviet territory on May 5.
- The pilot, **Francis Gary Powers,** was captured but later released.

Theme 13 DECADE OF CHANGE:
THE 1960s

*M*any issues and problems became matters of national concern during the 1960s: racial and gender inequality, economic deprivation, the limits of the Cold War containment strategy. This era of protest and upheaval owed its origins to demographic and cultural shifts, such as the entrance of baby boomers into colleges and the black exodus from the South. Social and political turmoil scarred the decade.

Key 68 Kennedy's New Frontier

OVERVIEW *John F. Kennedy brought energy and initiative to the presidency. His charisma and style energized Americans and made them optimistic about the future in spite of the existence of communism in the world and of poverty in America.*

Election of 1960: Eisenhower's vice president, **Richard M. Nixon,** was defeated in a close election by his Democratic opponent, **John F. Kennedy,** a senator from Massachusetts (1953–60) and a former congressman (1947–53).
* The major election issues concerned foreign affairs and the question of whether America's economic growth was proceeding at a satisfactory rate.
* Kennedy received 49.9 percent of the popular vote.
* He was the first Catholic president, and his religion was an issue in the election.

Kennedy-Nixon debates: Series of four televised debates that aided Kennedy's presidential candidacy.
* Kennedy looked and acted vigorous and self-confident.
* Nixon, who was recovering from an illness, appeared unshaved and haggard.

New Frontier: A term given to Kennedy's program of domestic legislation.
* The program consisted of aid to public schools, wilderness preservation, federal investment in mass transportation, and medical insurance for the elderly, funded by Social Security.
* Legislative initiatives met opposition in Congress.
* Bright, ambitious advisers and academics, attracted by the program, joined the administration, which believed that the federal government should be active, strong, and visible, with the president setting the tone.

Housing Act of 1961: Allotted federal grant money to cities for mass transit, subsidization of middle-income housing, and preservation of open space.

Economic policies: These involved tariffs, taxes, and inflation.
* Kennedy initiated tariff negotiations with foreign governments to stimulate American exports.

- In 1962 he proposed a federal tax cut to stimulate the economy.
- To control inflation, he pressured U.S. Steel to abandon its plans for price increases. Although his effort was temporarily successful, several months later the steel companies raised prices.

National Aeronautics and Space Administration (NASA): Created to undertake space exploration and put an astronaut on the moon which was accomplished by the Apollo 11 Mission in 1969.

Peace Corps: Funded by Congress in 1961; its first director was **Sargent Shriver.**
- Open to women and men of all ages, it was designed to assist people in developing nations.
- It helped promote goodwill and U.S. ideals.
- Volunteers, who served for 2–3 years, received an allowance to meet basic needs and maintain their health.

Kennedy assassination (November 22, 1963): Thinking ahead to his reelection in 1964, Kennedy went to Dallas for a political appearance.
- Riding in a motorcade, he was struck by two bullets and died a half-hour later.
- **Lee Harvey Oswald,** accused killer of the president, was later shot by **Jack Ruby.**
- For 4 days, Americans watched the events associated with the presidential funeral unfold.
- Chief Justice **Earl Warren** directed an investigation of the killing, which uncovered no evidence of a conspiracy. It resulted in the **Warren Commission Report.**
- The assassination has continued to stir controversy.

KEY QUOTATION

Ask not what your country can do for you; ask what you can do for your country.

John F. Kennedy
Inaugural speech, 1961

Key 69 Foreign policy under Kennedy

OVERVIEW *The Cold War mentality, particularly the doctrine of containment, characterized the decade, as evidenced by the Vietnam War. The United States believed that it must resist communism wherever it appeared. Effects of this policy included enhanced power of the president, continued growth of the military-industrial complex, larger defense budgets, and growing deficits.*

"Flexible response": A defense strategy under the Kennedy administration, which emphasized strengthening the tools of war and creating new ones. It held that a myriad of weapons could deter any type of war.

Alliance for Progress (1961): Fostered a series of projects, jointly undertaken by the United States and Latin American nations, to encourage economic development in Latin America and thus prevent the spread of communism.

Berlin Wall (1961): To curtail the exodus of East Berliners to West Berlin, the Soviet Union directed East Germany to build a wall between East and West Berlin. It symbolized the tension between the United States and the U.S.S.R.

Bay of Pigs (April 17, 1961): An attack on Cuba, which proved a great embarrassment to the United States. Begun under Eisenhower, it sought to eliminate Castro and communism.
  • The CIA trained an army of anti-Castro Cuban exiles in Central America.
  • They were transported to the Bay of Pigs in Cuba for an invasion of that country, which was expected to meet with popular support.
  • Its failure is attributed to two factors: Kennedy decided not to supply air support, and the Cuban people did not rise up to support the invaders.
  • Castro's forces crushed the invaders in two days.

Cuban missile crisis (October 1962): American intelligence sources and aerial reconnaissance photos uncovered evidence that Soviet missiles were being set up in Cuba.

- Kennedy set up a naval and air blockade around Cuba.
- While an American air attack on the missile sites was being considered, Soviet premier Khrushchev sent Kennedy a message implying that the missiles would be removed if America pledged not to invade Cuba.
- Kennedy agreed and privately promised to remove U.S. missiles from Turkey as well.
- The two nations had retreated from the brink of war.
- In November 1962, Russia agreed to dismantle all its missile bases in Cuba.

Nuclear Test Ban Treaty (1963): In this initial step toward mutual arms reduction, the United States and the U.S.S.R. agreed to ban the testing of nuclear weapons in the atmosphere.

Turmoil in the Dominican Republic: Power struggles followed the 1961 assassination of General **Rafael Trujillo.**
- American troops were sent there in 1965 to prevent the establishment of a pro-Castro, Communist regime.
- Forces were withdrawn after a conservative, Joaquin Balaguer, took control.

Key 70 Johnson's Great Society

OVERVIEW *Although Kennedy's accomplishments were meager and were cut short by his assassination, President Lyndon B. Johnson, through his genius for compromise, implemented many of Kennedy's plans and all that Truman had outlined in 1946.*

Election of 1964: Democrat **Lyndon B. Johnson,** vice president under Kennedy, was challenged by **Barry Goldwater,** an Arizona senator and the Republican nominee.
- Johnson offered a liberal agenda; Goldwater, a conservative, campaigned against expanding federal power in the economy and in civil rights.
- Johnson won 61 percent of the popular vote, one of the great landslides in American history.

Volunteers in Service to America (VISTA) (1964): As a domestic "Peace Corps," it was created by Johnson as part of the **Office of Economic Opportunity.**

Twenty-fourth Amendment (1964): Outlawed the **poll tax,** which had been used in the South to prevent blacks from voting.

Civil Rights Act (1964): Prohibited discrimination by employers and unions and guaranteed equal access to schools and public accommodations.
- Created the **Equal Opportunity Commission** to prevent job discrimination due to religion, national origin, race, or sex.
- Granted new powers to the U.S. attorney general to enforce these rights.

Kennedy-Johnson tax cut (1964): The economy was stimulated by a tax cut proposed by Kennedy in 1962 and enacted in 1964.

Great Society: Term applied to President Johnson's domestic program of the 1960s. Its top priority was his **"war on poverty."**
- **The Economic Opportunity Act (1964)** set up the **Office of Economic Opportunity.** Programs included;
  1. **Operation Head Start** (aiding preschoolers from underprivileged homes)
  2. **Job Corps** (for dropouts)
  3. **Neighborhood Youth Corps** (for unemployed teens)

4. **Upward Bound** (assisting low-income teens to aspire to college)
5. Other programs targeting rural areas and encouraging urbanites to help themselves (e.g., **Model Cities Program**).

- The New Deal Social Security programs now included other groups of workers (e.g., waitresses), and benefits were raised and tied to the cost of living.
- The **Department of Housing and Urban Development** was created to focus on cities.
- New environmental legislation sought to improve the quality of water and air.
- With the tax increase of 1967, a 10 percent surcharge to curb inflation, came a $6 billion reduction in funding for Great Society programs.
- By this point the Vietnam War had affected the economy.

Health Care Plans: Programs included:
- **Medicare (1965):** Funded through Social Security payroll taxes, it is a health plan for workers over 65, whether retired or still employed.
- **Medicaid (1965):** Funded by taxes, it is a health plan for welfare recipients.

National Endowment for the Arts (1965): Supports performing and creative arts programs.

National Endowment for the Humanities (1965): Supports projects that interpret America's cultural and historical heritage.

Elementary and Secondary Education Act (1965): Allocated $1 billion in federal funds to impoverished children attending Catholic schools.

Voting Rights Act (1965): Authorized the attorney general to send federal examiners to the South to register voters. Literacy and other voter qualification tests in states or counties were outlawed.

Immigration Act (1965): Limited the number of new immigrants to 170,000 per year. While immigration from some parts of Latin America was still restricted, people from Asia, Europe, and Africa could enter the United States on an equal basis.

Civil Rights Act (1968): Prohibited discrimination in the sale or rental of housing. Imposed penalties on people who injured civil rights workers and on persons who traveled from state to state to organize riots.

Key 71 The Vietnam War unfolds

OVERVIEW *By the late 1950s, after the French loss in 1954 and the failure to hold promised free elections in 1955, civil war raged between North and South Vietnam. President Johnson chose to escalate U.S. involvement during the 1960s after Kennedy's initial use of advisers.*

Situation in Vietnam during the 1950s and early 1960s: The United States had become involved in the civil war.
- Communist guerrillas had organized the **National Front for the Liberation of South Vietnam (NLF)** which had ties to the Communist government of the North.
- South Vietnam leader **Ngo Dinh Diem** asked for U.S. assistance and military aid.
- Between 1955 and 1961, 650 military advisers were sent to South Vietnam.
- Kennedy increased such military assistance, and 15,500 military personnel were sent to South Vietnam.
- The United States instigated a coup whereby military leaders took over the government.
- Diem and his associates were killed.

Johnson's Vietnam policy after Kennedy's assassination: Influenced by his foreign policy advisers, Johnson believed that the United States had an obligation to resist communism in Vietnam, and therefore escalated involvement in the war. Initially he sent 5,000 military advisers.

Gulf of Tonkin Resolution (1964): Passed by Congress, it became the legal means for escalation of the conflict, allowing the president to "take all necessary measures" to protect American forces and "prevent further aggression" in South Asia.
- The resolution was a response to an unprovoked attack by North Vietnamese torpedo boats on American destroyers in the **Gulf of Tonkin.**
- Doubts were later raised as to whether this act of aggression had actually taken place.

Bombing of North Vietnam (1965): After Communist forces attacked an American base at Pleiku and seven marines died, Johnson ordered bombing of the North.

- Such bombing raids continued until 1972.
- They had little effect, however, in limiting North Vietnamese assistance to the NLF.

Troop strength: 100,000 U.S. troops were in South Vietnam by 1965, and 500,000 were there by 1967. The quest for victory in Vietnam, considered to be vital to U.S. national security and prestige, had intensified.

"Pacification" and "relocation": As the war dragged on and victory seemed unattainable, two strategies were implemented:
- *Pacification* called for routing the Vietcong (Communist guerrilla forces in South Vietnam) from an area and then winning over the people.
- This strategy gave way to *relocation*, which involved removing villagers from their homes, sending them to camps or to the cities, and then destroying the countryside.
- In spite of these measures, victory remained elusive.

Antiwar movement: By 1967, the Vietnam War had taken center stage in the United States.
- Initially, intellectuals and students debated U.S. involvement in the war.
- Then pacifist organizations became involved.
- Campus demonstrations and peace marches materialized.
- In 1966, congressional hearings criticized the war.
- Even America's allies voiced their distaste for U.S. involvement.

Tet offensive (1968): An attack on U.S. strongholds throughout South Vietnam by the **Vietcong.**
- The episode eventually developed into a military victory for the United States.
- Media coverage of it, however, stirred significant U.S. antiwar sentiment and tarnished Johnson's popularity.

Key 72 Struggle for racial equality

OVERVIEW *The crusade for civil rights became a nation-wide cause during the 1960s. Blacks won political and legal rights, and segregation was largely abolished.*

"Sit-Ins": On February 1, 1960, four black college students sat at the "whites only" counter in a Woolworth store in Greensboro, North Carolina, and refused to move.
- This sit-in tactic spread to other areas of the South.
- To coordinate other sit-ins, the **Student Nonviolent Coordinating Committee (SNCC),** led by **Stokely Carmichael,** was formed.

"Freedom rides": During 1961, an interracial group, the **Congress of Racial Equality (CORE),** organized "freedom rides" on interstate buses traveling from Washington, D.C. to New Orleans.
- Blacks and whites challenged the segregation of buses, rest rooms, and restaurants and violence often erupted.
- The **Interstate Commerce Commission** ordered all interstate vehicles and terminals to be desegregated.

James Meredith (October 1962): When the University of Mississippi refused to admit him, a federal court ordered that he be enrolled.
- Governor **Ross Barnett,** a segregationist, refused to enforce the order.
- Kennedy sent federal troops to the city after rioting by whites, in defiance of the court decree, occurred.

Governor George Wallace (1963): To prevent a court-ordered enroll-ment of several black students at the University of Alabama, he blocked the doorway. The students were admitted after federal mar-shals arrived.

March on Washington (August 1963): Over half a million blacks and whites, representing black and white organizations, marched to the Lincoln Memorial in Washington, D.C.

"Freedom summer" (1964): A major voter registration drive in the South.
- One episode exemplified the acts of violence that characterized this latter phase of the civil rights movement.
  1. Three volunteers (**James Chaney, Andrew Goodman,** and **Michael Schwerner)** disappeared from Philadelphia, Missis-sippi, in June 1964.

2. They had been murdered by members of the Ku Klux Klan.
3. The perpetrators were eventually caught, tried, and convicted by a federal court.
- By 1970, black voters had become a force in Southern politics.

Malcolm X: A leader of the **Black Muslim movement** whose ideology advocated black nationalism, not integration, he was killed in 1965 by a rival Muslim faction in New York City.

"Black power": An ideology that emphasized a range of feelings from black self-reliance to violent revolution, all emphasizing less cooperation with white society.
- Black power leaders included the SNCC's Stokely Carmichael and **H. Rap Brown.**
- At the extreme end of the spectrum was **Huey Newton,** leader of the militant **Black Panthers.**
- After this shift to militancy, whites played a minor role in the civil rights movement.
- The black power movement encouraged the growth of racial pride in black America, of "black studies" in schools and colleges, and of new black literacy and artistic movements.

"Affirmative action": Supported by President Lyndon B. Johnson in 1965, it recruited blacks for jobs to compensate for past injustices.
- In 1968, the Department of Labor ruled that every contractor doing business with the federal government must submit "a written affirmative action compliance program."
- Such guidelines eventually applied to any business or institution receiving money from or doing business with the federal government.

Urban riots (1967–68): Occurring in about 75 cities, they allegedly resulted from poverty, unemployment, police brutality, and white control of business and real estate. In particular, the assassination of Dr. Martin Luther King, Jr., in Memphis, Tennessee, on April 4, 1968, by **James Earl Ray,** kindled rioting in 40 cities.

KEY QUOTATION

I have a dream that one day . . . the sons of former slaves and the sons of former slave-owners will be able to sit together at the table of brotherhood.

Dr. Martin Luther King, Jr.
March on Washington, 1963

Key 73 Minority equal rights

OVERVIEW *The civil rights movement also inspired Hispanics, Native Americans, and gays to agitate for equality and individual "liberation."*

Hispanics: Several groups emerged to promote their interests.
- **Mexican-American Political Association,** which helped to elect Kennedy.
- **Brown Berets,** a militant organization modeled on the Black Panthers.
- **La Raza Unida,** which promoted Hispanic candidates for public offices.
- **United Farm Workers,** a union representing migrant farm workers led by **Cesar Chavez,** which conducted massive boycotts in California.

Native Americans: They had the worst housing, disease rates, and education levels of any group in American society.
- The **American Indian Movement (AIM),** created during the 1960s, used black power tactics. In Washington, D.C., its members occupied the Bureau of Indian Affairs and later Wounded Knee, South Dakota, site of an 1890 Sioux massacre by U.S. soldiers.
- Lawsuits were filed against citizens in a variety of states in attempts to reclaim Indian lands taken in violation of treaties or federal laws.
- The **Declaration of Indian Purpose (1961):** was issued by 67 tribes in Chicago who sought to preserve their heritage.
- The **National Indian Youth Council** promoted Indian nationalism and intertribal unity.
- The **Indian Civil Rights Act (1968)** recognized tribal laws as legitimate within reservations and guaranteed Indians on reservations rights as stipulated in the Bill of Rights.

Gay liberation movement (1969): This began in New York City, with the "Stonewall riot," in which gay patrons of a gay bar in Greenwich Village fought back against harassment by police.
- Gays sought social acceptance as well as political and economic rights.
- The **Gay Liberation Front** was founded in New York.
- Beginning in 1974, with the election of Elaine Noble to the Massachusetts legislature, openly gay politicians won election to various offices.
- Democrats began to include gay rights in their party platforms.

Key 74 Feminism

OVERVIEW *Social and demographic changes sparked the New Feminism, which ultimately caused fundamental changes in women's lives.*

Origins of the New Feminism: Factors contributing to the revival of feminism included:
- Betty Friedan's *The Feminine Mystique.*
- Kennedy's **President's Commission on the Status of Women,** which brought gender discrimination in education and employment to the public's attention and assisted in the creation of networks of feminist activists.
- Woman's experiences in the civil rights movement, the antiwar movement, and the New Left, which led them to organize for women's liberation.

Equal Pay Act (1963): Passed in Kennedy's administration, the act prohibited paying women less than men for equal work. Other legal protections were included in Title VII of the 1964 Civil Rights Act.

National Organization for Women (1966): Established by Betty Friedan and other feminists, it sought to attain equality of opportunity and freedom of choice for all women. In short, it advocated economic and legal equality.

Women's liberation: In its extreme form, the movement rejected marriage, family, and heterosexual intercourse.
- It encouraged women to assault male power.
- Such radical views were expressed in **Kate Millett's** *Sexual Politics* (1969) and **Shulameth Firestone's** *The Dialectic of Sex* (1970).
- The movement sparked the creation of grassroots organizations and activities that carried on the battle against sexism.

"Consciousness raising": A technique of the women's liberation movement.
- It utilized group sessions where women shared their experiences in growing up female.
- These discussions made women aware of shared societal oppression.

Equal Rights Amendment (ERA): Approved in 1972, but never ratified by three-fourths of the states. Even a 3-year extension, granted

171

by Congress for its ratification, was not long enough, and the amendment died.

Abortion: Although previously illegal, abortion was eventually legalized because of pressure by the women's movement.
- The *Roe* v. *Wade* decision in 1973 allowed abortion during the first trimester.
- This Supreme Court decision was based on the constitutional right to privacy.

Effects of the New Feminism: These included:
- **Affirmative Action Plan (1970)** initiated by President Johnson as an executive order in 1965, later extended the guidelines to include women.
- The title **Ms.** replaced Mrs. or Miss in business, deemphasizing a woman's martial status in the working world.
- The **two-career family** became the norm by the 1970s as wives sought careers and often postponed motherhood. Living expenses were such that two wage earners were needed.
- More women entered the professions.
- More women were elected to political office.
- Women routinely hold Cabinet positions.
- In 1981 **Sandra Day O'Connor** became the first female justice of the Supreme Court.
- **Geraldine Ferraro** of New York was the Democratic Party's vice-presidential candidate in 1984.
- In 1983 **Sally Ride** became the first woman astronaut to go into space.
- Women's sports received more recognition and prize money.
- Women's studies became a flourishing field in colleges and universities across the nation.
- The **Equal Credit Opportunity Act (1975)** prohibited banks or other lenders from discriminating on the basis of gender.
- **Title IX of the Educational Amendments Act of 1972** prohibited colleges and universities that received federal funds from discriminating on the basis of sex.

KEY QUOTATION

Equality of rights under the law shall not be denied or abridged by the Untied States or any state on the basis of sex.

Equal Rights Amendment
Never enacted into law

Key 75 The New Left and the counterculture

OVERVIEW *The social upheavals of the 1960s challenged traditional middle-class American values. The politically conscious New Left and the antiestablishment counterculture emerged.*

New Left: Young men and women who were civil rights and antiwar activists during the 1960s and advocated more radical political beliefs after the civil rights movement had experienced a Southern backlash.

Students for a Democratic Society (SDS) (1962): An organization founded by 40 white youths in Michigan.
- Issued the **Port Huron Statement,** summarizing their political objectives.
- Envisioned a new community of "the people" that would end the Vietnam War, secure economic and racial justice, and change the political system.

Free speech movement (1964): This movement of the rights of students to pursue on-campus political activities began at the University of California at Berkeley.
- As a result, the ban on political solicitation on campus was removed.
- Protests encompassed the depersonalization of higher education and the existence of corrupt public policies.
- Columbia and Harvard students seized college buildings, and violence often ensued.
- A few cases of arson and bombing occurred, orchestrated by the **Weathermen,** an offshoot of SDS.

"Teach-ins": First organized by faculty and students at the University of Michigan and later spreading to other campuses, they were designed to discuss the political, moral, and diplomatic aspects of U.S. involvement in Vietnam and to inform others about these issues.

Antiwar movement: The New Left's most successful crusade.
- Stimulated by the end of automatic student deferments in 1966, student activists organized several large political demonstrations to protest the Vietnam War.

1. March on the Pentagon, October 1967.
2. The **"spring mobilization"** of April 1968.
3. The Vietnam **"moratorium"** of November 1969.
- Campus rallies often include draft card burnings.
- Campus recruitment by the military and the CIA brought on-campus protests, accompanied by violence. College administrators often utilized local police officers to quell disturbances.
- Some young people evaded the draft by moving to Sweden or Canada, or accepted jail sentences as a form of civil disobedience.

Campus strikes and killings: After President Nixon announced a U.S.-backed invasion of Cambodia in 1970, a national student strike was organized.
- At **Kent State** (Ohio), on May 4, 1970, National Guardsmen fired into a crowd of students, killing four and wounding eleven.
- At **Jackson State College** (Mississippi), two students died.
- By May, over 400 colleges were closed because of strikes.

Counterculture: Exhibited dislike for society through an alternative lifestyle that included long hair, drug use, and permissive sexual behavior.

Hippies: Individuals who followed the social behavior of the counterculture.
- Many looked to the beat poets and writers of the 1950s as their role models.
- They dominated the **Haight-Ashbury** neighborhood of San Francisco and New York's **East Village.**
- Many lived on rural communes across the United States.
- They valued a simpler, natural existence and the idea of personal fulfillment.
- They considered modern society dehumanizing.

Woodstock Music Festival (August 1969): Typified the appeal of rock music to the new generation of the 1960s.
- More than 400,000 young people attended this concert, which lasted several days and featured major rock performers.
- Participants indulged in drugs and sex as they "got high" on music.

Impact of the counterculture: Effects took various forms:
- The counterculture was reflected in mainstream America via hair styles, clothing, language, and behavior.
- Films and television began to examine political issues, violence, social conflict, and sexual mores.
- The greatest effect lay in spreading the message of social and political unrest through rock music.

Theme 14 LEADERSHIP IN CRISIS

*I*n response to the social unrest of the early 1960s, the end of the decade was characterized by a call for social order. Public attention turned to inflation, declining productivity, and limited growth. Concern about the economy was coupled with the crisis in authority precipitated by the Watergate affair. When President Nixon resigned in 1974, public respect for authority had reached a new low.

Key 76 A turning point—the 1968 election

OVERVIEW *Richard Nixon sought the presidency in 1968. At that time the Democratic Party was in disarray after President Lyndon Johnson's announcement that he would not seek or accept renomination.*

Johnson's withdrawal (March 31, 1968): Since his showing in the primaries was poor, President Johnson announced that he would not seek reelection for president and declared a halt to the bombing of North Vietnam.

Eugene McCarthy: A Minnesota senator who entered the Democratic presidential primaries as an antiwar candidate.
- He drew support from many young people and mobilized concern about the Vietnam War.
- He became a serious contender for the Democratic presidential primary, but failed to win the nomination.

Robert F. Kennedy and his assassination (June 5, 1968): As one of the Democratic contenders for the presidential nomination, Kennedy defeated Eugene McCarthy in the California primary.
- A young Palestinian, **Sirhan Sirhan,** opposed Kennedy's pro-Israel stand.
- Shortly after Kennedy had given a victory speech, Sirhan shot him in the head as he was leaving the ballroom of a Los Angeles hotel. Kennedy died shortly thereafter.

Chicago Riot (August 28, 1968): While the Democratic national convention met, Chicago police fought with antiwar demonstrators.
- The scene was televised nationwide and showed police using billy clubs, mace, and tear gas.
- The protests were part of a building resentment and distrust of the Johnson administration policies in Vietnam.

Election of 1968: Voters were offered a choice of three candidates.
- A disunited Democratic Party chose Vice-President **Hubert H. Humphrey** as its candidate. Humphrey disassociated himself from Johnson's war effort, but identified himself with his domestic policies.
  1. Seen as a middle-of-the-road candidate.

2. Had a strong record on civil rights.
- **Richard M. Nixon,** as the Republican candidate, made a remarkable political comeback from his defeats in the 1960 presidential election and the 1962 California gubernatorial election.
    1. He portrayed himself as the representative of the **"silent majority."**
    2. He promised **"peace with honor"** in Vietnam, law and order at home, and smaller government.
    3. He received 43 percent of the popular vote and won the election.
- A third party candidate, Governor **George C. Wallace** of Alabama, appealed to some conservative voters. He denounced forced busing of students, black riots, student protests, and antiwar demonstrations.
    1. His campaign slogan called for law and order.
    2. He claimed allegiance to the interests of the poor.

Key 77 Nixon's domestic policy

OVERVIEW *President Nixon sought to balance the needs of the poor with those of the middle class. Also, he attempted to reduce federal interference in local affairs.*

"New Federalism": Nixon's policy to balance the power of the federal government and the interests of local communities. Programs would allow the power and resources of Washington to flow back to the states and their localities.

Curtailment of federal programs: Funding was reduced or cut off for many social programs, and in 1973 the Office of Economic Opportunity was abolished.

"Stagflation": Term used to denote an economic condition characterized by high prices and low demand, such as prevailed throughout the 1970s.

Economic Stabilization Act (1970): Imposed a 90-day freeze on all wages and prices.
- Phase II of Nixon's economic plan mandated guidelines for wage and price increases, administered under a federal agency.
- Phase III made wage and price controls flexible and largely voluntary.

Moon landing (July 1969): Fulfilling the promise of John F. Kennedy to place a man on the moon by the end of the decade, the United States achieved its goal.
- Astronauts **Mike Collins, Neil Armstrong,** and **Edwin Aldrin,** in **Apollo 11,** landed on the moon.
- Neil Armstrong's first steps on the lunar surface were televised. Later President Nixon was viewed by millions speaking with the astronauts by telephone.
- Samples of moon rocks were brought back to earth.
- Costs of the space program brought differences of opinion regarding its worth when weighed against domestic problems.

Environmental awareness: Related to the energy crisis was a growing public concern for environmental protection.
- The pesticide DDT was banned in 1969 by the Agriculture Department.
- The **Clean Air Act** was passed in 1970.

- The **Environmental Protection Agency** and the **Occupational Safety and Health Administration** were created in 1970.
- The **Resource Recovery Act,** approved in 1970, provided money for states and cities to build solid-waste disposal systems to recycle salvageable materials.
- Development of supersonic air transport was dropped by Congress in 1971.
- The **Clean Water Act** was approved in 1972.

Spiro T. Agnew's resignation: On October 11, 1973, Agnew resigned as vice president of the United States.
- While governor of Maryland, he had taken bribes from contractors and had even received "kickbacks" as vice president.
- Charged with income tax evasion and extortion, he pleaded no contest.
- In addition to resigning as vice president, he was fined $10,000, disbarred as a lawyer, and placed on three years' probation.
- Under the terms of the **Twenty-fifth Amendment,** which provided for presidential succession, Nixon nominated **Gerald R. Ford,** a Republican congressman from Michigan, as vice president.

KEY QUOTATION

One small step for man, one giant step for mankind.

Astronaut Neil Armstrong
Apollo 11 mission, moon landing, July 1969

Key 78   The Supreme Court:

Liberalism versus

conservatism

OVERVIEW *The Nixon administration sought to curb the civil liberties trend of the Supreme Court established during the late 1950s and early 1960s.*

Warren Court decisions: The Warren Court advocated civil liberties and alienated many Americans by its decisions.
- *Engel v. Vitale* **(1962):** Prayers in public schools were ruled unconstitutional, based on the separation of church and state in the First Amendment.
- *Baker v. Carr* **(1962):** State legislatures must apportion representation so that votes of all citizens carry equal weight. This decision established the "one person, one vote" rule.
- *Gideon v. Wainwright* **(1963):** The precedent that, regardless of ability to pay, every felony defendant is entitled to the Sixth Amendment right to a lawyer was established.
- *Escobedo v. Illinois* **(1964):** A defendant must be allowed access to a lawyer before being questioned by police.
- *Miranda v. Arizona* **(1966):** Authorities must inform criminal suspects of their Fifth and Sixth Amendment rights.

"Burger" or "Nixon" Court decisions: After the resignation of Chief Justice **Earl Warren,** Nixon appointed conservative-minded **Warren Burger** to lead the Court.
- Under Burger, the Supreme Court actually extended social reform.
  1. *Swann v. Charlotte-Meckenburg Board of Education* **(1971):** Supported forced busing to achieve racial balance in schools.
  2. *Furman v. Georgia* **(1972):** Created guidelines for Eighth Amendment capital punishment laws.
  3. *Roe v. Wade* **(1973):** Legalized abortion during the first trimester.
- *Milliken v. Bradley* **(1974):** Ruled that busing would not take place across district lines.
  1. The concept that suburban and city schools had to be combined to achieve racial balance was rejected.
  2. Violence occurred in Boston between 1974 and 1976 over court-ordered busing.

- ***Bakke* v. *University of California* (1978):** Absolute quotas were declared illegal.
  1. The Court ordered that Allen Bakke be admitted to the University of California at Davis Medical School.
  2. It upheld the principle of affirmative action, however, by ruling that racial factors could be considered in hiring or in admission decisions.

Key 79 Nixon and the war
in Vietnam

OVERVIEW *President Nixon pursued a foreign policy that sought a more stable world. He ended the war in Vietnam.*

Henry Kissinger: As Nixon's National Security Council chief and later as secretary of state, he was instrumental in shaping and implementing Nixon's foreign policy initiatives.

Vietnamization: Nixon's policy for winding down the war.
- It consisted of training and equipping the South Vietnamese military to replace U.S. forces.
- In 1969, 60,000 U.S. ground troops were withdrawn from Vietnam.
- By 1972, only 24,200 U.S. troops remained in Vietnam.
- This strategy undermined opposition to the war.

Widening war: While troop strength was being reduced in Vietnam, bombing raids over North Vietnam and neighboring countries increased.
- In 1969, Nixon ordered secret bombing raids of neutral Cambodia.
- During the spring of 1970, U.S. ground forces invaded Cambodia to destroy enemy troop sanctuaries. This action, announced by Nixon on television, sparked widespread antiwar protests.
- In December 1970, Congress repealed the **Gulf of Tonkin Resolution.**
- Nixon ordered the air force into Laos to assist the South Vietnamese forces in 1971.
- The South Vietnamese army retreated within a few weeks reeling from their defeat in Laos.
- Bombing of Vietnam and Cambodia continued, and by 1972 it was escalated again in response to a North Vietnamese offensive.
- In addition, seven North Vietnamese harbors were mined.

Pentagon papers: Leaked to the press by former Department of Defense official Daniel Ellsberg, they revealed that the government had been dishonest in reporting the military progress of the war and in detailing its motives for U.S. involvement.
- Excerpts appeared in *The New York Times* and in other papers in 1971.
- The Supreme Court upheld the publication of the papers.

Lieutenant William Calley: Tried and convicted, in 1971, of overseeing the massacre of over 100 unarmed South Vietnamese civilians. The case exemplified the dehumanizing impact of the war.

Twenty-sixth Amendment (1971): Gave 18-year-olds the right to vote. This amendment was widely supported because the average age of U.S. personnel dying in Vietnam was 19, younger than those in Korea.

"Peace with honor": During the summer and fall of 1972, Kissinger had been meeting with the North Vietnamese foreign secretary, **Le Duc Tuo,** in Paris, to arrange a cease-fire.
- When talks broke off in December, 12 days of bombing North Vietnamese cities resulted.
- Talks resumed, and on January 27, 1973, an agreement ending the war was signed by the United States, North Vietnam, South Vietnam, and the "Provisional Republican Government" of the South.

Paris Accords: The peace agreement that ended the Vietnam War.
- Provisions included a cease-fire and release of several hundred American prisoners of war by the North Vietnamese.
- Provisions did not include a stipulation for withdrawal of North Vietnamese troops from the South or the abandonment of the Communist commitment to a reunified Vietnam.

Aftermath of the accords: The situation in Southeast Asia was as follows:
- Communist forces controlled most of Laos.
- The bombing of Communist havens in Cambodia ceased in August 1973.
- By 1975, Communist forces overran the South, occupied Saigon, and renamed it Ho Chi Minh City.
- Vietnam had been reunited under communism.
- Cambodia fell to communism as well.
- U.S. involvement in Vietnam resulted in the deaths of 1.2 million Vietnamese soldiers and over 57,000 Americans.

The War Powers Act (1973): Required the president to report use of military force to Congress within 48 hours and directed the end of involvement within 60 days unless Congress declared war.

Key 80 Foreign policy under Nixon

OVERVIEW *With Kissinger, Richard Nixon reconceptualized older foreign policy assumptions. Both recognized that the world was now dominated by three power centers—America, Europe, and Japan. The administration sought accommodation with the Soviet Union and the recognition of China as a significant world power.*

Detente: Under Nixon, a relaxation of tensions between Communist nations and the United States took place.

Nixon Doctrine (1969): This policy statement was designed to avoid involvement in another Vietnam.
- The United States would honor its treaty commitments, including economic and military aid.
- Nations threatened by internal subversion or nonnuclear aggression should provide for their own defense.
- This provision meant troop reduction in Korea and an agreement to return Okinawa to the Japanese.

Relations with China: Henry Kissinger was sent on a secret mission to Beijing in July 1971.
- By October 1971, China had been admitted to the United Nations, and Taiwan expelled.
- In February 1972, Nixon made a week-long visit to China
- In 1973, the two nations established "liaison offices" in Washington and Beijing that were, in effect, embassies.
- This new relationship was designed to use China as a wedge against the U.S.S.R.

SALT talks: These discussions took place in Helsinki, beginning in 1969 and resulted in **SALT I,** a **Strategic Arms Limitation Treaty** between the United States and the U.S.S.R.
- This accord limited the construction of antiballistic missile systems (ABMs).
- Each nation agreed to limit itself to its existing number of intercontinental ballistic missiles (ICBMs).
- After Nixon's visit to Moscow to sign the agreement, a Soviet-American wheat deal and other trade agreements were made.

Latin America (1970–73): The United States poured money into Chile to undermine its elected Marxist president, **Salvador Allende.**

- He was murdered shortly after he lost power in 1973.
- The new repressive government received military and economic support from the United States.

Middle East: During the **Six-Day War** of 1967, Israeli forces defeated Arab armies and seized territory from Egypt, Jordan, and Syria.
- Thereafter, Palestinian Arab refugees fomented instability in Jordan and Lebanon.
- Egyptian and Syrian forces attacked Israel in October 1973.
- After 10 days of fighting, the United States pressed for a cease-fire to what has become known as the **Yom Kippur War.**
- U.S. dependence on Arab oil forced a consideration of Arab interests in this region.

Key 81 The Watergate crisis

OVERVIEW *By 1973, a crisis in authority was precipitated by an attempted cover-up of a break-in of Democratic headquarters at the Watergate Hotel. When President Nixon resigned in 1974, the public respect for authority had reached a new low.*

Election of 1972: Incumbent President **Richard M. Nixon** defeated his Democratic opponent, South Dakota Senator **George S. McGovern,** by receiving 61 percent of the popular vote. The people found Nixon's proposals appealing: advancing traditional values, restraining social reform, decentralizing political power, balancing international relations.

George Wallace: He received strong support in some early Democratic primaries, but in May 1972 was shot and seriously wounded at a rally in Maryland.

Senator George S. McGovern: Charging that the Nixon administration had corruptly abused its power, the Democratic presidential nominee was an outspoken critic of the Vietnam War.
  * He also took a liberal stance on most social and economic issues.
  * He lost support by changing running mates.
    1. Senator **Thomas F. Eagleton,** from Missouri, was asked to leave the ticket after it was revealed that he had undergone electroshock therapy for nervous depression.
    2. Eagleton was replaced by **Sargent Shriver.**

White House paranoia: Nixon's first administration had been marked by secrecy and mistrust.
  * **Cambodia bombing:** In early 1969, *The New York Times* published an exposé of America's secret bombing raids in Cambodia.
  * Fearing further leaks of information, the White House set up illegal wiretaps of newspeople and the National Security Council.
  * **Pentagon papers:** In an attempt to find damaging evidence to discredit **Daniel Ellsberg,** the Defense Department analyst who helped to publicize American blunders during the Tet offensive of 1968, the White House approved the burglarizing of his psychiatrist's office.

The **"plumbers": G. Gordon Liddy** and **Howard Hunt** were hired by the White House to plug leaks of government material.

Watergate break-in: On June 17, 1972, five men were arrested at the headquarters of the **Democratic National Committee** in the Watergate Hotel in Washington, D.C.

- The five burglars who were arrested had several accomplices, including security consultants in the White House and a member of the **Committee to Re-Elect the President (CREEP).**
- *Washington Post* reporters **Robert Woodward** and **Carl Bernstein** helped uncover much of the incident.

Cover-up: Nixon's top assistant, **H. R. Haldeman,** was ordered to have the CIA stop FBI probes that connected the burglars with the White House.

Nixon resignation: In May 1973, former Nixon aide **John Dean** implicated President Nixon in the cover-up before a Senate committee, chaired by Senator **Sam Ervin** of North Carolina.

- Tape recordings of White House conversations could implicate Nixon. Invoking his executive privilege, he refused to release them.
- On July 30, 1974, the House of Representatives voted three articles of impeachment: obstruction of justice, abuse of power, and subverting the Constitution.
- On August 5, 1974, Nixon released the tapes upon orders of the Supreme Court. They revealed his part in a cover-up attempt beginning 6 days after the break-in.
- On August 9, 1974, Nixon resigned the presidency. One month later, President Gerald R. Ford pardoned his predecessor.

Impact of Watergate: Congress passed two acts:

- **Fair Campaign Practices Act of 1974** demanded stricter accounting of campaign expenditures and limited campaign contributions.
- **Freedom of Information Act of 1974** strengthened the act of 1966, providing citizens with greater access to any files the government may have collected on them and permitted photocopying of the contents by interested persons.
- **Privacy Act of 1974** allowed citizens the right to examine government agency files collected on them.

Theme 15 TOWARD A
CONSERVATIVE
AMERICA

*A*fter Watergate a new, more conservative mood characterized the United States. Traditional and moral values, including evangelical religion, became embodied in political life. On the economic side, Americans continued to struggle with inflation, unemployment, high energy costs, a trade deficit, and a burgeoning federal deficit. Politicians promised a smaller role for the federal government, along with a decreased bureaucracy and less spending.

Key 82   Ford's domestic and
foreign policies

OVERVIEW *Gerald R. Ford attempted to rebuild confidence in the presidency and energize the economy. In both endeavors, his success was limited.*

Vice president and cabinet: Ford nominated former New York Governor **Nelson A. Rockefeller** as his vice president, and the nomination was confirmed in December 1974.
- **Henry Kissinger** remained as secretary of state.
- Most other members of Nixon's cabinet also retained their posts.

The Nixon pardon: Ford's pardon of Nixon after only a month in office heightened speculation concerning a deal between the two. It also hurt Ford's reputation for integrity, his credibility, and his popularity.

Energy crisis (1973–74): Sparked by the **Oil and Petroleum Exporting Countries' (OPEC)** embargo imposed on the United States and its allies because of their support of Israel during the **Yom Kippur War** of 1973.
- OPEC nations also raised oil prices 400 percent in 1974.
- The resulting gas shortage changed American driving habits, and a nationwide speed limit of 55 miles per hour was instituted.

Recession (1974–75): OPEC price increases and government spending for the Vietnam War touched off an inflation rate of almost 12 percent in 1974. The severe recession was also caused by the Ford administration's policies: advocating high interest rates, vetoing federal spending increases, and resisting an increase in taxes.

Ford meets Brezhnev (1974): The two leaders signed an arms control agreement at Vladivostok in Siberia.
- The agreement served as the basis for SALT II.
- It imposed a ceiling on the number of ICBMs (intercontinental ballistic missiles) launched from submarines of multiple independently targeted reentry vehicles (MIRVs) and bombers capable of hitting targets over 6,000 miles away.

CIA report (1975): Vice President Rockefeller was appointed by President Ford to examine alleged CIA abuses.

- The report revealed that since the 1940s the CIA had been involved in clandestine domestic activities, an area closed to its jurisdiction.
- It possessed intelligence files on 300,000 Americans.
- Its activities included break-ins, illegal wiretaps, and mail interceptions.

Helsinki Accords (1975): The Soviet Union, the United States, and other Western nations legitimized the borders drawn in Eastern Europe after World War II. The Soviet Union and its satellites signed a "human rights" guarantee, which included the right to emigrate.

Middle East: Henry Kissinger orchestrated an agreement between Israel and Egypt.
- It stated that force would not be used to resolve their differences.
- Israel pledged to return portions of the occupied Sinai to Egypt.

Mayaguez **(1975):** This U.S. merchant ship, with a crew of 39, was captured by Cambodian forces in the Gulf of Siam.
- When negotiations failed to release crew members, Ford sent in U.S. forces.
- Although the crew were freed, over 80 marines were killed or wounded.

Election of 1976: Republican Gerald Ford chose conservative Senator **Robert J. Dole** of Kansas as his running mate against former Governor of Georgia **James ("Jimmy") Earl Carter.**
- In the campaign Republicans defended Ford's honesty and fiscal restraint in government.
- Carter promised full employment, support for social programs, and a balanced budget.
- As an outsider, he pledged to return morality to government.
- Carter emerged victorious with 50 percent of the popular vote.
- He gained a majority of the electoral votes, 297, including the entire South with the exception of Virginia to Gerald R. Ford's 240.

Key 83 The Carter administration

OVERVIEW *Although one of the most intelligent presidents, Jimmy Carter was also one of the most unpopular. He attempted to identify with the common person, but problems with the economy and energy shortages overshadowed his presidency. In addition, although a Democrat, he had trouble developing good relations with the Democratic Congress, and eventually was saddled with a hostage crisis that led to his downfall. As the incumbent, he failed in his bid for reelection.*

Economic problems and measures: Carter reduced unemployment by increasing public spending for public works and services and by cutting federal taxes.
- He appointed conservative economists **G. William Miller** and **Paul Volcker** to head the **Federal Reserve Board.**
- Nevertheless, by 1980, interest rates hovered around 20 percent, money was tight, and prices were rising at an annual rate of more than 10 percent.

Fuel shortage: In 1979 the fuel situation worsened.
- Another oil embargo resulted in long lines at gasoline stations.
- OPEC announced another major price increase, and consequently the prices of natural gas, coal, kerosene, and home heating fuel rose.

Deregulation under Carter: His administration supported decontrol of oil and gas prices to spark domestic production and encourage energy conservation, thereby slowing inflation and rising prices.
- The **Airline Deregulation Act (1978)** provided for the elimination of the Civil Aeronautics Board over six years, the free entry of airlines into new routes, and competition in regard to air fares.
- The **Motor Carrier Act (1980)** gradually withdrew the government from controlling access, rates, and routes in the trucking industry.
- The **Rail Act (1980)** allowed railroad executives to negotiate mergers with barge and truck lines.
- The **Depository Institutions Deregulation and Monetary Control Act (1980)** permitted savings and commercial banks to write

home mortgages, extend commercial loans, and underwrite securities issues. Ceilings on interest rates were removed.

Human rights: The defense of human rights became the basis for U.S. foreign policy under Carter.
- He created an **Office of Human Rights** within the State Department.
- American economic and military aid was withdrawn from countries that violated human rights.
- Carter spoke out against the suppression of dissent in the Soviet Union.

Panama Canal: The Senate ratified treaties negotiated by Carter regarding the future of the Panama Canal.
- The United States would gradually hand over control of the Canal Zone to Panama.
- Panama agreed to maintain the canal's neutrality.
- The United States retained the right to send ships through the canal in case of war.

Camp David Accords: In 1977, Egyptian President **Anwar el Sadat** accepted an invitation to visit Israel from Israeli Prime Minister **Menachem Begin.**
- Sadat proclaimed that Egypt would accept Israel as a legitimate political entity.
- To facilitate further negotiations, Carter invited both leaders to a summit conference at Camp David in September 1978.
- After two weeks, they announced an agreement on a "framework" for an Egyptian-Israeli peace treaty.
- After postponing a resolution of the Palestinian refugee problem, Begin and Sadat returned to the White House and signed a formal peace treaty on March 26, 1979; this was Carter's greatest foreign policy accomplishment.

China: On December 15, 1978, the United States and China issued a joint message declaring that formal diplomatic relations between the two nations would be restored on January 1, 1979.

Afghanistan: Soviet troops invaded Afghanistan on December 27, 1979.
- Carter viewed the action as a prelude to control over the world's oil supplies.
- Economic sanctions were imposed on the Soviet Union.
- U.S. athletes were not allowed to participate in the **1980 Summer Olympic Games** in Moscow.
- In 1978, Carter had met with **Brezhnev** to complete a new SALT II arms control agreement, which limited the number of

long-range missiles, nuclear warheads, and bombers for both nations. The administration now withdrew the **SALT II** treaty from Senate consideration.

Iran hostages: In January 1979, the **Shah of Iran** left his country.

- His repressive, authoritarian ways and efforts to modernize and westernize Iran had produced a Moslem fundamentalist revolutionary movement led by **Ayatollah Khomeini.**
- In October 1979, the Shah entered the United States to receive cancer therapy in a New York hospital.
- In response, an armed mob entered the American embassy in Teheran on November 4, and took diplomatic and military personnel as hostages.
- If the Shah was returned to Iran to stand trial for crimes against the Iranian people, the hostages would be released.
- Although a few were released, 53 Americans were held in the embassy for over a year.
- Carter imposed economic sanctions and got the United Nations to condemn the taking of American hostages.
- After talks regarding the hostages broke off in April 1980, Carter ordered a secret rescue mission, which ended in failure, to free the prisoners.
- Until the end of his term, Carter held talks with Iran and agreed to release several billion dollars in frozen Iranian assets in exchange for the hostages.
- As Ronald Reagan assumed the presidency on January 20, 1981, word came that the hostages were returning to the United States after 444 days in captivity.
- Homecoming for the hostages was marked by grand displays of patriotism.

Key 84   American life in the 1970s and 1980s

OVERVIEW   *The conservative outlook of this period was a response to the social and cultural changes of the 1960s.*

Demographic changes: The "graying" of America was among the noticeable trends of the 1970s and 1980s.
- Higher life expectancy and a declining birth rate contributed to this trend.
- Men and women married later and postponed having children because of career pressures.
- In 1980, the average household had 2.75 people, down from 3.1 in 1970.
- Those having children had fewer because of financial constraints (e.g., higher housing costs).
- The legalization of abortion, along with contraceptive and sterilization procedures, also curbed the birth rate.
- Other trends included:
  1. An increase in the percentage of households headed by women—from 10.2 percent in 1970 to 17.5 percent in 1980.
  2. An increase in the divorce rate—from 3.5 divorces per 1,000 persons in 1970 to 5.2 divorces per 1,000 in 1980.

New immigration: The period from 1970 to 1990 witnessed the largest migration of people to America in the twentieth century.
- A growing Hispanic (from Latin America) and Asian (from Korea, India, and Southeast Asia) presence characterized this immigration.
- The **Immigration Reform and Control Act (1987)** required employers to confirm the legal status of their employees or face economic and possibly criminal penalties.
- Undocumented workers who had entered the United States before 1982 were offered amnesty.
- Asian Americans experienced resentment from other Americans because of their strong work ethic; they also excelled in education.

"Sun belt" migration: By 1980, more Americans lived in the Southeast and Southwest than in the North and East. Many industries and corporate headquarters relocated there.

Gentrification: During the 1980s, many "yuppies" (young urban professionals) purchased real estate in the cities, refurbished it, and established prosperous new urban communities.

- This process, called gentrification, attracted new businesses to the cities.
- It also restored a viable tax base.
- This process resulted in the displacement of the poor as well.

Cities: American cities were generally on the decline in this period.
- Poor housing, increasing violence, drug addiction, and inferior schools characterized urban areas.
- Services and tax revenues shrank.

Drug abuse: Sparked by the introduction of "crack" cocaine, the illegal drug trade became enormously profitable.
- Violence ravaged most cities as drug trafficking fed crime.
- Even a high official—Washington, D.C., Mayor **Marion Barry**—was convicted of a cocaine-possession misdemeanor in 1990.

AIDS epidemic: Related to the drug epidemic is acquired immune deficiency syndrome (AIDS), the product of a virus transmitted by the exchange of body fluids, which attacks the immune system.
- Although the first victims of this incurable disease were homosexual men, the most rapid increase in its spread has occurred among intravenous drug users.
- The virus is spread by sharing contaminated needles, through sexual intercourse with an infected partner, and through blood transfusions with contaminated blood.

Homelessness: A tragic trend of the 1980s, homelessness resulted from rising housing costs, cuts in federal support for public housing, reduced welfare assistance, fewer unskilled jobs, and the increase in family instability, as well as the deinstitutionalizing of the mentally ill.

"Underclass": Term used to describe the growing number of black families (one-third) and Hispanic families (one-fourth) living in poverty. By contrast, less than 11 percent of white families were classified as poor.

Gay rights: During the 1980s, in some cities and states, gays won rights enjoyed by heterosexuals.
- Many cities banned job discrimination against homosexuals.
- In 1982, Wisconsin and 11 other states expanded their civil rights laws to make sexual orientation a protected category.
- Almost 100 cities and several corporations offered health insurance and other benefits to domestic partners.
- The Vermont legislature created the category "civil unions" for same-sex couples, enabling them to enjoy rights available to married couples regarding inheritance, taxes, and medical decisions.

Key 85 Emerging political views

OVERVIEW *While the social and cultural changes of the 1960s affected life-trends in the 1970s and 1980s, political views galvanized in the form of continued efforts to create change and a backlash of political conservatism.*

Right wing: This political right consisted of middle- and lower-class Americans, many of whom were evangelical Christians, who were concerned about social and cultural, rather than economic, issues.
- During this period it was a significant force within the Republican party and included some Democrats as well.
- It publicized "family" issues, campaigned against the Equal Rights Amendment, and attacked feminism.
- **Phyllis Schlafly,** a New Right leader, organized the **stop ERA movement.**

Rise of evangelical Christianity: Although various cults and pseudo-faiths were popular during the 1970s and 1980s, the major religious revival in the United States involved evangelical Christianity.
- During the 1980s, over 70 million Americans were "born-again" Christians.
- They established newspapers, magazines, radio stations, schools, colleges, and cable television networks.
- Even President Carter said that he was a "born-again" Christian.

Moral Majority: Led by the Reverend **Jerry Falwell,** a Baptist minister from Roanoke, Virginia, this political organization was created in 1979.
- It sought to obtain the passage of federal laws to restrict abortion, to curtail crime, pornography, and drugs, and to reinstitute prayers in public schools.
- Many also urged the teaching of creationism in schools and sought stricter censorship of television, movies, and books.
- This conservative message gained strength through the highly successful television ministries of Falwell, **Pat Robertson,** and **Oral Roberts.**
- The Moral Majority was dissolved in 1989 after **Jim Bakker's** fraud conviction and the revelation of Jimmy Swaggart's sexual improprieties. Both were leading evangelical ministers.

Right-to-life movement: Organized during this period, primarily by Catholics, it sought to end legalized abortions. Its members consider fetuses to be human beings who have a "right to life" from the moment of conception.

Abortion issue: In 1976, Congress passed an amendment barring the use of Medicaid funds to pay for abortions for poor women, even if a physician deemed the procedure medically necessary.
- It was upheld by the Supreme Court in *Harris* **v.** *McRae* (1980).
- In *Webster* **v.** *Reproductive Health Services* (1989), a Missouri law forbidding any institution from receiving state funds for performing abortions (whether or not those funds were used to finance abortions) was upheld.
- The **pro-choice movement** emerged during the 1980s to defend a woman's right to choose whether and when to bear a child. Polls indicated that most Americans supported this position.

Activists on the left: They advocated saving the environment, limiting economic development, and halting the production of nuclear weapons and power plants.
- A militant antinuclear movement emerged in the late 1970s.
- Followers opposed new nuclear plant construction and sought to educate others about the dangers of existing plants.

Three Mile Island (March 1979): One of more than 42 nuclear plants in the United States, located near Harrisburg, Pennsylvania.
- The plant's central core reactor came close to a meltdown, which would have released dangerous levels of radioactive material into the environment.
- This incident bolstered the antinuclear movement begun in the 1970s.

Antinuclear movement: Coalesced between 1981 and 1983 and then faded.
- It sought to stop the spread of nuclear weapons and to promote world disarmament.
- Some members demanded disarmament negotiations, others advocated a "nuclear freeze" (halting production of nuclear systems or weapons), and a third group called for a commitment to "no first use" of atomic weapons.

Environmental movement: The first nationwide "Earth Day" in 1970 marked the beginning of the environmental movement.
- Environmentalists contend that all elements of the earth's environment are intimately and delicately linked together.
- When the balance in one element is upset (e.g., by toxic waste and pollution), other elements risk damage.
- Economics is less important than ecological health.

- Scientists argue that society poses a danger to the natural world by the release of industrial pollutants, particularly **chlorofluorocarbons,** into the atmosphere, thereby depleting the ozone layer that protects the earth from the sun's most dangerous rays.
- Scientists also discuss **global warming,** a rise in the earth's temperature resulting from emissions produced by the burning of fossil fuels.

Key 86 Reagan's New Federalism

OVERVIEW *President Ronald Reagan moved toward a conservative New Federalism policy. Although he changed the priorities of the national government and curbed its expansion, he did not reduce its size or scope.*

Image: Although the oldest man to serve as president, Reagan cultivated a vigorous public image.
- He continually appealed to the public through television and public appearances.
- His Hollywood image and nationalistic rhetoric proved to be extremely popular.

The New Right: A broad, loose coalition of conservatives, "Reagan Democrats," and those appalled by the liberal social, economic, and political trends of the 1960s and 1970s.
- Supported free markets.
- Opposed government intervention in people's lives.
- Believed that Christian civilization was being threatened by the high divorce rate, rise in illegitimate births, use of drugs, easily available abortions, pornography, feminist ideology, and gay rights activists.

The election of 1980: New groups became Republican party members: "Reagan Democrats," Southern whites, affluent ethnic suburban Catholics, and young conservative voters. Right-wing support helped Reagan win.
- His campaign promises included stricter laws against crime, drugs, and pornography, opposition of the federal government to easy-access abortions, a reverse from the retreat he saw the United States taking throughout the world, and increased defense spending.
- **John B. Anderson,** congressman from Illinois, ran as an independent third-party candidate.
- Ronald Reagan defeated **Jimmy Carter,** the Democratic incumbent, by receiving almost 51 percent of the popular vote.

Assassination attempt: On March 31, 1981, Reagan, along with his press secretary, **James Brady,** was shot and wounded by **John Hinkley** outside a Washington, D.C. hotel.

Supreme Court appointee: In 1981, Reagan nominated **Sandra Day O'Connor** of Arizona as the first woman Supreme Court Justice. She was confirmed by the Senate shortly thereafter.

Reagan deregulation: He lessened or abolished governmental control on the environment, health care, the workplace, and the consumer. Agencies targeted included the Environmental Protection Agency, the Occupational Safety and Health Administration, and the Consumer Product Safety Commission.

Election of 1984: Reagan won a landslide victory with 59 percent of the popular vote over Democratic challenger **Walter Mondale,** vice president under Carter. Mondale chose as his running mate New York congresswoman **Geraldine Ferraro,** the first woman ever to be included on a national presidential ticket.

Key 87 Reagan's economic policy

OVERVIEW *President Reagan sought to lower taxes, decrease spending for domestic programs, increase expenditures for the military, and restore U.S. international competitiveness.*

"Reaganomics": Reagan declared in his inaugural address that "government is the problem" regarding the economy.
- He stated that government was a swollen bureaucracy and that national security made it necessary to fight "the enemies of freedom."
- He cut domestic programs (health, housing, food stamps, school lunches, environmental protection, the National Endowment in the Arts and Humanities) by $35 billion.
- He added $12.3 billion in defense spending.
- The Economic Recovery Tax Act (see below) cut personal income taxes by 25 percent.
- His critics called this approach "voodoo economics."

Economic Recovery Tax Act (ERTA) (1981): Cut taxes but favored the wealthy.
- It provided for a three-year rate reduction on both individual and corporate taxes.
- It did not redistribute income at the lower end.
- Cuts in the federal budget accompanied the tax cut.

1982 recession: Unemployment rose to 10.7 percent, the highest level since the 1930s.
- Inflation declined to 4 percent.
- Economic recovery resulted in part from the tax cuts of 1981, which stimulated spending.

Response to the deficit: The budget deficits during the Reagan years were larger than any that the U.S. government had accumulated in its entire previous history.
- The United States became the world's largest debtor nation.
- Much of the deficit resulted from the 1981 tax cuts and the increase in military spending.
- Reagan responded by raising Social Security taxes and by cutting domestic spending for programs such as food stamps, low income housing, school lunches, and student loans.

Gramm-Rudman (Balanced Budget and Emergency Deficit Reduction Control) Act (1985): Required a balanced budget by 1991.
- Mandated major deficit reductions over five years.
- Provided for automatic budget cuts in all areas of government spending if the president and Congress were unable to agree on a compromise.

The Child Support Enforcement amendments: Facilitated collection of court-ordered child support payments from absent parents.

The Retirement Equity Act (1984): Strengthened divorced and widowed women's claims to their husbands' pensions and enabled women to qualify more easily for private retirement pensions.

Tax Reform Act of 1986: Aimed to simplify the tax codes and reduce the highest tax brackets.
- Stimulated saving and investment.
- Eliminated certain tax shelters.

Savings and loan industry: As controls over savings and loan institutions were reduced, speculation and often personal corruption affected the industry. By 1990, the government was forced to act to prevent the collapse of many banks.

Scandals: Improper behavior and activities in government came to light during Reagan's administration.
- Funds were misused by the Department of Housing and Urban Development.
- Several appointees close to Reagan left office.
  1. The secretary of labor was indicted for racketeering. He was later acquitted.
  2. The White House counsel and later attorney general compromised his office.
  3. When it was revealed that CIA and Defense Department officials had carried out questionable stock transactions, they resigned.
- Officials of the Environmental Protection Agency resigned when it was revealed that they were not enforcing that agency's regulations.

The stock market and corporate takeovers: On October 19, 1987, the U.S. stock market experienced an historic first; its greatest single-day decline.
- A financial innovation of the decade, the "leverage buyout," had resulted in many corporate takeovers, and several corporations declared bankruptcy.

- Many takeovers were facilitated by issuing "junk bonds," high-risk, high-interest loan instruments.
- The market for such bonds collapsed during the 1980s.
- In 1989, the most powerful junk bond trader, **Michael Milken,** was indicted. His company, **Drexel, Burnham, Lambert,** collapsed in 1990.

Key 88 Reagan's foreign policy

OVERVIEW *The basis of Ronald Reagan's policy was the belief that all discord throughout the world was caused by the Soviet Union.*

Reagan Doctrine: Signaled American activism in the Third World. The United States would support opponents of communism anywhere in the world.

Nicaragua: The **Sandinistas,** led by **Daniel Ortega,** overthrew **Anastasio Somoza** in 1979.
- Reagan believed that the Soviet Union and Cuba were backing this pro-Communist group.
- He supplied guns, food, uniforms, and military advisers to the guerrilla forces, the **Contras,** to help them overthrow the Sandinistas.

Iran-Contra affair: In 1986 the Reagan administration revealed that it had secretly negotiated with Iran to secure the release of several American hostages held in the Middle East.
- Moreover, the United States had sold arms to Iran in exchange for its assistance.
- Part of the arms deal money was secretly placed in a fund to aid the Contras in Nicaragua.
- Congressional hearings revealed that a "secret government" existed, dedicated to promoting the administration's foreign policy goals through covert and often illegal means.
- Such activity was unknown to the Defense Department, the State Department, and possibly the CIA.
- The prominent figure in this "government" was Marine Lieutenant Colonel **Oliver North,** a staff member of the National Security Council, who was fired by Reagan in November 1986.
- The investigations never linked Reagan to the most serious violations of the law.
- North, Admiral **John Poindexter,** a national security adviser, and **Robert McFarlane,** a former national security adviser, were indicted for violating various federal laws.

Grenada: In October 1982, American soldiers and marines were sent to the Caribbean island of Grenada to overthrow an anti-American Marxist government friendly to the Soviet Union.

- This action also served to protect American medical students.
- This brief invasion was very popular with the U.S. public.

El Salvador: This nation struggled with left-wing revolutionaries, supposedly supported by Cuba and the U.S.S.R. Reagan increased military and economic aid while insisting that U.S. forces would not be sent there.

Middle East: United States support for Israel was weakened, and troops were pulled out of Lebanon.
- Support for Israel decreased when it invaded Lebanon in 1982 to destroy **Palestinian Liberation Organization** bases.
- In 1983, 241 American marines on a peace-keeping mission in Lebanon were killed when a car bomb driven by an Islamic fundamentalist exploded under the marine barracks.

Libya and terrorism: In 1986, Reagan ordered the bombing of sites in Tripoli, Libya's capital, to punish terrorism.
- Libya's leader, **Muammar al-Qaddafi,** was believed to be a leading sponsor of terrorism.
- Throughout the 1980s, terrorist acts took place on airplanes and cruise ships, and in airports and commercial and diplomatic posts.
- American and other Western hostages were also seized.
- In October 1985, four Arabs seized an Italian cruise ship, *Achille Lauro,* in the Mediterranean, killed a disabled Jewish-American tourist, and tossed his body into the sea.
  1. They surrendered to Egypt on condition they would be provided with safe passage to Libya on an Egyptian airliner.
  2. American F-14 jets were ordered to intercept the airliner. It landed in Italy and the terrorists were taken into custody.
- After a Libyan-planned bombing of a West German club frequented by American military personnel, Reagan initiated an air strike against Libyan bases from British airfields.

Poland: When the Polish government put down the rebellion by **Solidarity,** an anti-Communist Polish trade union movement led by Lech Walesa, Reagan imposed sanctions on the Soviet Union. Walesa wanted to improve working conditions through economic reform.

Missile build-up: By the early 1980s, both the Soviet Union and the United States had placed new intermediate-range missiles in Europe.
- Reagan announced a **Strategic Defense Initiative (SDI),** dubbed "star wars" by critics, which would make nuclear war obsolete by its capability of intercepting missiles in space to prevent an intercontinental missile attack.

- The Soviets ended arms limitation talks after the United States placed Pershing missiles on launch pads in West Germany.

Mikhail Gorbachev: After he assumed the leadership of the Soviet Union in 1985, U.S.–Soviet tensions were reduced.
- He introduced two new policies:
    1. **Glasnost** involved the elimination of many repressive policies: Soviet citizens could speak freely, organize politically, and criticize the government.
    2. **Perestroika** called for the modification of the Soviet economy by employing private ownership and the profit motive.
- In 1986, Reagan and Gorbachev met in Reykjavick, Iceland, to discuss mutual reduction of their nuclear arsenals.
- In 1988, they signed a treaty eliminating American and Soviet intermediate-range nuclear forces (INFs) from Europe.
- Also in 1988, Moscow withdrew its troops from Afghanistan.

China: Reagan moved toward closer ties with mainland China.
- In 1984, Reagan visited Peking and signed new agreements for the sale of nuclear power plants to the People's Republic.
- Reagan pledged to reduce arms shipments to Taiwan.

KEY QUOTATION

The Soviet Union was an evil empire (and the conflict with the United States) . . . a struggle between right and wrong, good and evil.

Ronald Reagan on the Soviet Union

Key 89 The Bush presidency

OVERVIEW *Although George Bush made many preelection promises concerning the national deficit, education, drug abuse, crime, homelessness, the environment, poverty, and world peace, he was unable to accomplish much without cooperation from the Democratic Congress.*

Election of 1988: After Reagan's two-term presidency, Vice President **George Bush** won the Republican nomination and chose Senator **Dan Quayle** of Indiana as his running mate.
- The Democratic nominee was Massachusetts Governor **Michael Dukakis,** with Texas Senator **Lloyd Bentsen** as the vice presidential candidate.
- Bush ran a largely negative campaign, accusing Dukakis of being "soft" on crime and holding liberal views, while defending the accomplishments of the Reagan administration.
- He advocated an end to legalized abortion and asserted that the disadvantaged could receive assistance through "a thousand points of light" (i.e., private charity).
- He received 54 percent of the popular vote.

Flag burning: The Supreme Court held that flag burning is symbolic speech, protected by the Bill of Rights.
- Bush sponsored an amendment to the Constitution that would ban flag burning.
- The amendment was defeated in Congress.

Abortion issue: The *Roe v. Wade* decision of 1973 was modified by two later decisions:
- *Webster v. Reproductive Health Services, Inc.* (1989) permitted the State of Missouri to place conditions on abortion.
- *Planned Parenthood v. Casey* (1992) permitted states to restrict abortion as long as the restriction did not place an "undue burden" on a woman.

Savings and loan scandal: Many Americans lost money in failed savings banks.
- By 1990, the savings and loan (S&L) system appeared to be on the verge of bankruptcy.
- Congress established an agency to take over the S&Ls, rescue cheated depositors, and oversee the sell-off of remaining assets.

- It was revealed that many congressmen had received favors from S&L lobbies to support an easing of federal restrictions.
- Moreover, President Bush's son Neil was involved in dubious deals with one large, failed S&L.
- The extent of the fraud, waste, and incompetence angered Americans, who, as taxpayers, bore the burden of the bailout.

Americans with Disabilities Act (1990): Prohibited discrimination against Americans with physical or mental disabilities.

Reauthorization of the Clean Air Act (1990): Required businesses to control emissions of nitrogen oxides and sulfur dioxide. Bush's Council on Competitiveness, headed by Vice President Dan Quayle, undercut this act and other environmental regulations on the grounds that they slowed economic growth and cost jobs. The Justice Department overruled the Environmental Protection Agency when it sought to prosecute large corporate polluters.

Education: Although Bush proclaimed that by the year 2000 American students would rank second to none in math and science, his means to achieve this goal involved only promoting government vouchers parents could use to pay tuition at public or private schools of their choice.

Reversal on taxes: The ever-increasing budget deficit and the general economic climate convinced Bush that new taxation was imperative.
- He called for additional revenues in a budget conference of congressional leaders in 1990.
- In November 1990, after a five-month struggle, a compromise $492-billion budget bill was signed by President Bush. The bill raised taxes, especially for middle-income people, and resulted in a new tax code and new income-tax rates being issued.
- A prolonged economic recession began in 1990, the deepest since the Great Depression.
- The nationwide shrinkage of the work force resulted from corporate "restructuring" and "downsizing," which affected large numbers of white collar workers.
- The unemployment rate was more than 7 percent by 1992.

Clarence Thomas hearings (1991): Senate hearings to confirm **Clarence Thomas's** appointment to the Supreme Court to replace **Thurgood Marshall** were bitter and nationally divisive.
- Reagan had appointed Thomas, a black conservative, to head the Equal Employment Opportunity Commission (EEOC).
- Black civil rights and women's organizations were concerned about his conservative record, and at the hearings Thomas successfully skirted controversial topics (e.g., abortion).

- As the hearings continued, **Anita Hill,** a law professor at the University of Oklahoma, revealed that Thomas had sexually harassed her when he was her superior at the Department of Education and at the EEOC.
- Thomas denied the charges, which were aired publicly.
- He was confirmed by the Senate, amid this controversy, by a vote of 52 to 48.
- The episode politicized the confirmation process, raising serious questions regarding the hearings.

L.A. riot and Rodney King (April 1992): When a California jury acquitted four police officers charged with beating Rodney King, a black motorist, the bloodiest urban riot since those in the 1960s took place.
- Forty-five people died and 2,000 were injured, and much of the city burned.
- Bush supported emergency aid but did not address the racial and urban problems connected with the riot.

27th Amendment (ratified May 18, 1992): Prohibited congressional pay raises from taking effect until an election had seated a new session of Congress.
- A reaction to a congressional pay raise coupled with disclosures regarding the mismanagement of the House bank.
  1. Representatives had written thousands of bad checks that the bank covered at no fee.

Pardon of Iran-Contra figures (1992): Bush pardoned former Secretary of Defense Caspar Weinberger and other Iran-Contra players who had been indicted on felony counts for lying to Congress and obstructing a congressional inquiry before he left office.

Election of 1992: President George Bush, the incumbent, failed to be reelected to a second term.
- A harsh and lingering recession, with unemployment above 8 percent and the national debt at $4 trillion, formed the backdrop to the campaign.
- His Democratic opponent, Arkansas Governor **Bill Clinton,** was victorious, despite being called an adulterer and a draft dodger.
  1. Before the New Hampshire primary, it was reported that while governor, Clinton had an affair with Gennifer Flowers, which she confirmed days later.
  2. The Clintons appeared on CBS's "60 Minutes" and denied the allegations, but then he issued a vague appeal for forgiveness to Americans directly.
  3. This revelation failed to damage his election as the Democratic Party's candidate for president in the November election.

- The campaign focused not only on character, but on family values and the economy. Each party emphasized the importance of family, but the Clinton/Gore ticket promised "people for a change."
  1. Clinton vowed to reform health insurance and the welfare system, while controlling the budget deficit and stimulating the economy.
- These pro-choice "baby-boomers" received 43 percent of the popular vote.
- President-elect Clinton and his Vice President-elect and former Tennessee Senator **Al Gore,** became the youngest ticket in American history.
- The Independent Party candidate, Texas billionaire **Ross Perot,** received almost 20 percent of the popular vote. This was the highest percentage received by a third party candidate since Theodore Roosevelt ran on the Bull Moose ticket 80 years ago.
  1. He waged a grass roots campaign which sought to get his name on the ballot in every state. In July 1992, he withdrew from the race but by September he was back.
  2. His candidacy emphasized passing the American dream onto America's children by presenting a five-year plan for balancing the budget. He promised to serve without pay if elected and to break the gridlock between the president and Congress.
  3. His platform included cutting government spending by eliminating waste, getting rid of restrictions on American business, and restructuring the health care system. He supported gun control and abortion and promised to get rid of political action committees and "foreign lobbyists."
- This election had a 55 percent voter turnout, the highest since the 1976 election.
- The Democrats controlled both houses of Congress, which seated 39 African-Americans, 19 Hispanic-Americans, seven Asian-Americans, one Native American, and 48 women including the first African-American woman, Carol Moseley Braun, as a U.S. senator.

KEY QUOTATION

Read my lips: no new taxes.

George Bush
Campaign pledge, 1988

Key 90 Foreign policy under President Bush

OVERVIEW *In regard to foreign affairs, President Bush seemed to be in the right place at the right time: communism and the Cold War came to an end, the Soviet Union disintegrated, and Operation Desert Storm became America's greatest military triumph since World War II.*

Panama: In 1989, American troops were sent to Panama to overthrow **Manuel Noriega,** under indictment in the United States for drug trafficking.
- Captured, he stood trial in the United States and in 1992 was convicted of helping the world's most infamous drug cartel to smuggle cocaine into the United States from 1981 to 1986.
- A pro-American civilian government was elected to replace him in Panama.

Nicaragua: In 1990, the **Sandinistas** lost the Nicaraguan elections. The struggle between the **Contras,** who had received military aid under Reagan, and the Sandinistas had a peaceful outcome.

China (1989): Student demonstrators called for democratization, and demonstrations continued after Gorbachev's visit to Beijing in 1989.
- Increasing numbers of Chinese supported such protests, and the Communist government felt threatened.
- Hard-line leaders took control and military forces entered Tiananmen Square in Beijing on June 3, 1989.
- Thousands died and repression resulted.
- After the incident, Bush sent two aides to China to restore cordial relations with the government.

South Africa: In 1990, major opposition movements by blacks, particularly the **African National Congress (ANC),** were legalized.
- This was a move toward ending white supremacy through the apartheid system.
- After 27 years in prison, the ANC leader, **Nelson Mandela,** was released.

End of communism: Mikhail Gorbachev's policies of glasnost and perestroika sparked nationalist movements in several Soviet republics during 1989.

- Non-Communist governments appeared in Eastern Europe: Poland, Czechoslovakia, Bulgaria, Hungary, Romania, and East Germany.
- Demonstrators tore down the Berlin Wall.
- In 1990, in consultation with the United States, France, Great Britain, and the Soviet Union, German Chancellor **Helmut Kohl** merged the two Germanys economically and politically after promising economic aid to the Soviet Union.
- On August 18, 1991, a coup resulted in the downfall of the Communist party and in the birth of the Commonwealth of Independent States (CIS).
- President Boris Yeltsin took over the leadership after Mikhail Gorbachev's resignation on December 25, 1991.
- The U.S. recognized the 12 new countries of the CIS and opened diplomatic relations with Russia, the Ukraine, Belorussia, Kazakhstan, Kirghizia, and Armenia.
- In 1992, the U.S. Senate ratified the START nuclear arms treaty between the United States and four republics of the former Soviet Union. The terms of the treaty reduced the number of nuclear weapons held by all.

Start I (1991): Russia and U.S. pact to reduce each other's nuclear warheads to 6,000 and each other's strategic delivery systems to 1,600.

Start II: Provided for the reduction of warheads to around 3,000 each by the year 2003 and the elimination of land-based intercontinental ballistic missiles (ICBMs) with more than one warhead, with each side having about 500 ICBMs.

Yugoslavia: In 1991, four of its six republics seceded. Serb minorities, backed by Serbia, incited civil wars in Croatia and Bosnia.
- In Bosnia, Muslims were driven from their homes and towns during "ethnic cleansing." Bush was criticized for failing to act decisively.

Operation Desert Shield (1990): When **Saddam Hussein** of Iraq invaded oil-rich Kuwait, there was international concern.
- Prompted by economic self-interest and the wishes of Saudi Arabia and Kuwait, Bush sent American troops to Saudi Arabia.
- Other United Nations members also sent troops, along with supplies and ships, to assist the Americans.
- Saddam Hussein took many civilians in Kuwait and Iraq prisoner, including Americans. They were released late in 1990.
- A meeting in Geneva between U.S. Secretary of State **James Baker** and Iraqi Foreign Minister **Tariq Aziz** failed to resolve the issue of the Iraqi invasion.

Operation Desert Storm (1991): Iraq refused to leave Kuwait by January 15, 1991, the UN-imposed deadline.

- Under the authority of the United Nations and the U.S. Congress, President Bush authorized a military attack on Iraq on January 16.
- Scud missile attacks were launched by Saddam Hussein against Saudi Arabia and major Israeli cities but U.S. pressure prevented Israeli retaliation.
- On February 24, coalition forces (American, British, French, and Arab troops) led a ground attack against the Iraqis.
- A cease-fire ended the fighting on February 28.
- Although Kuwait was now free of Iraqi forces, Saddam Hussein remained in power and later defied UN inspection teams.

Impact of Operation Desert Storm: A great display of patriotism characterized the war. American television presented minute-by-minute coverage, even though there was tight military censorship of the media.

Somalia: Collapse of the government in 1991 left the country in chaos. In 1992, Bush gained UN sanction for a military force led by American troops to restore peace and alleviate hunger.

KEY FIGURES

General Norman Schwarzkopf: He commanded the UN forces in the Middle East during Operation Desert Storm.

General Colin Powell: Chairman of the American Joint Chiefs of Staff, he was the first black to occupy that position.

Key 91 Clinton as president

OVERVIEW *As the nation's first baby boom president, the "New Democrat" Clinton promised change after 12 years of Republican rule. His administration faced many challenges, enjoyed the longest economic boom in American history, and a surplus in the federal budget. But his presidency culminated in the first presidential impeachment since Andrew Johnson in 1868.*

The Clinton administration: Clinton had marketed himself as a supporter of the middle class, who believed in restraining federal programs and budgets, being tough on crime, and valuing religion and family.
* His cabinet included the first woman attorney general, **Janet Reno,** and the first woman secretary of state, **Madeleine Albright,** former U.S. ambassador to the United Nations, appointed during his second term. **Donna Shalala,** former University of Wisconsin president, became the secretary of health and human services.
* He appointed **Ruth Bader Ginsberg,** a judge who believed abortion was constitutional, to the Supreme Court in 1993, along with **Stephen Breyer.**
* Of his first 129 appointments to federal courts, 11 were Hispanic, 31 were black, and almost one-third were women.

White House travel office scandal: Clinton fired several employees of this office, which led to a call for a special counsel to investigate the illegalities related to the firings.

Gays in the military: Clinton's policy called for a "don't ask, don't tell" philosophy. Instead of lifting the ban on homosexuals, it allowed dismissal of men and women who said they were gay or engaged in homosexual behavior. This policy resulted because of objections raised by the Joint Chiefs and a number of members of Congress.

Abortion: Clinton said he would veto any congressional bill limiting abortion rights.
* Clinton used his executive power to ease some of the restrictions on abortion counseling and the importation and use of RU-486, a French "abortion pill."
* The pill was approved by the FDA for distribution in 2000.

- Clinton also authorized the use of fetal tissue for research purposes.

Economic plan (1993): Passed by close votes and reduced the federal deficit to its lowest level in 10 years.
- Called for higher taxes for the middle class.
- Imposed a 10 percent surtax on individuals with taxable incomes over $250,000, an energy tax, and a higher corporate tax.
- Proposed to cut government spending via a smaller defense budget and a downsized bureaucracy.

Brady Bill (1993): Provided aid to municipalities for police, crime prevention programs, and the building of prisons.

Family and Medical Leave Act (1993): Allowed workers in larger companies to take unpaid leave of up to 12 weeks for childbirth, adoption, care of elderly parents, or family medical emergencies.

Waco, Texas (1993): Government agents stormed the Mt. Carmel compound of an apocalyptic sect, the **Branch Davidians.** Their leader, **David Koresh,** was a rock musician and a self-styled messiah. Following reports about the group stockpiling arms, violating immigration laws, abusing children, and engaging in false imprisonment, agents from the Treasury Department's Bureau of Alcohol, Tobacco and Firearms met gunfire as they attempted to enter the compound on February 28, 1993. Four agents and two Branch Davidians died, while about 20 people were injured. The FBI took over the siege and after 50 days of psychological warfare, attacked the compound. The compound caught fire and about 75 people died, including Koresh. Attorney General Janet Reno took responsibility for the decision to assault the compound.

Militia movement: After Waco, information about and popular interest in "militia" or "patriot" groups accelerated. Joining well-armed militia organizations reflected a belief that the federal government was conspiring against individual liberties, particularly the right to bear arms. Some groups promoted racial and ethnic hatred. Others supported right wing Christian groups, especially those who were militant antiabortionists. Many others refused to pay taxes, challenged the federal control of public lands, and threatened to arrest and execute local government and judicial officials.

Health care reform (September 1993): This health care reform plan was designed to help 39 million Americans without health insurance by providing universal coverage.
- The plan called for employers and employees to share the cost, 80 to 20 percent.

- Government would subsidize all or part of the payments for small businesses and the poor.
- Funds would come from Medicaid and a "sin tax" on tobacco and alcohol.
- First Lady **Hillary Rodham Clinton** chaired the health care plan task force.
- Plan would curb the rising costs of medical care.
- This "managed competition" plan was not approved after a year of congressional wrangling and the health care industry charged it would increase taxes and increase government interference in health care decisions.
- Private industry did make some progress in curtailing costs.
- In 1996, Congress did enact reform by allowing workers who changed jobs to keep health insurance.
- Congress established a new health care program for 5 million uninsured children.

1994 midterm elections: Republicans gained control of Congress for the first time in 40 years.
- Republicans also won majorities in 15 state legislatures and won a net gain of 11 governorships.
- Religious and social conservatives helped bring this Republican victory.
- The new speaker of the House, **Newt Gingrich,** a representative from Georgia, became a voice for the conservative right. He had challenged operations of the House bank and post office.
- The **Conservative right** issued a **"Contract with America,"** which called for congressional term limits, a balanced budget amendment, a presidential line-item budget veto, stricter penalties for violent criminals, welfare reforms, programs to strengthen families, increased defense spending, reduced government regulations, legal reforms to stop excessive liability claims, frivolous suits and "overzealous" lawyers, tax cuts, and an amendment to ban abortions.
- Clinton, fellow Democrats, and some moderate Republicans, opposed most of these contract pledges.
- The House brought all 10 initiatives to a vote within 100 days.
- The two items that became law were: Congress agreed that laws passed by the House must apply to House members as well as other Americans; Congress agreed to stop imposing mandated programs on local and state governments without footing the bill.
- Clinton's veto of the 1995 federal budget led to the virtual shutdown of the government, since the government ran out of money

and shut down all but essential services. Congress did not want to give in to Clinton's demands for changes in their proposed budget.

- The "contract" moved Clinton to change his agenda and message. **Dick Morris,** a Democrat turned Republican turned Democrat became a new chief advisor to Clinton and from 1995 to 1996 assisted him in moving closer to Republican positions on government regulation, welfare reform, and the budget deficit.

Violence Against Women Act (1994): Authorized $1.6 billion and new strategies for combating sexual assaults and domestic violence.

- The law was weakened when the Supreme Court invalidated a provision that allowed victims of gender violence to sue in federal court.

Anticrime Act (1994): Pushed by Clinton, it banned several types of assault weapons.

Oklahoma City bombing (April 19, 1995): On the second anniversary of the Waco incident, a federal building collapsed when a truck exploded outside it.

- 168 people died and more than 850 were injured.
- It was bombed by **Timothy McVeigh,** who was tried and convicted in 1997 and executed for the crime at age 33 in 2001, and **Terry Nichols.**
- It was America's first closed-circuit television broadcast of a federal death sentence.
- McVeigh claimed that he was enraged by federal efforts to restrict the sale of firearms and the federal government's actions in dealing with the Branch Davidians at Waco.

Racial issues:

Million Man March (October 16, 1995): Leader of the black separatist **Nation of Islam, Louis Farrakhan,** called on African-American men to show their solidarity by taking part in this march in Washington, D.C.

- About half a million participated.

Judicial conservatism: Since the 1980s, the Supreme Court has shifted to the right.

- It restricted federal affirmative action programs.
- It questioned the legality of election districts redrawn to create black or Hispanic districts.
- It limited legal remedies for racially segregated public schools.

Adarand Constructors v. *Pena* **(1995):** The court questioned the value and constitutionality of a government program that gave preferential treatment to businesses owned by "disadvantaged" minorities.

***Hopwood* v. *Texas* (1996):** a federal appeals court decision rejected the use of race as a factor in college admissions, even for the "wholesome practice" of producing racially balanced student bodies.

Proposition 209 (1996): In July 1995, the Regents of the University of California ordered an end to affirmative action.
- The next year, California voters abolished racial and gender preferences in all government hiring, education, and contracting under Proposition 209.
- Other states enacted similar laws.

Defense of Marriage Act (1996): Prohibited the federal government from recognizing state-licensed marriages between same-sex couples.

Personal Responsibility and Work Opportunity Reconciliation Act (1996):
- Abolished aid to families with dependent children and replaced it with grants to the states, with the requirement to limit welfare payments to two years whether the recipient could find work or not.
- Set a lifetime limit of aid at five years, barred legal immigrants who were not citizens from food stamps and other benefits, and allowed states to cut off **Medicaid** to legal immigrants.
- Required that at least half of a state's welfare recipients have jobs or be enrolled in job-training programs by 2002 or have their federal funds cut.

Other achievements:
- Approved an increase in the minimum wage.
- Made voter registration easier.
- Improved college students' access to federal loans.
- Established the **Americorps** program enabling students to pay for their education with community service.
- Pushed through an increase in the **Earned Income Tax Credit** for low wage earners. People who worked full-time for low wages received tax reductions.
  1. If they paid no taxes, they would receive a government subsidy to lift their family income above the poverty level.
- Passed a campaign finance reform bill.

Clinton's personal problems:
Whitewater (1994): Involved a 1978 Clinton investment in a resort project on Arkansas' White River. This investigation was sparked by the death of **Vince Foster,** deputy White House Counsel, in 1993. He allegedly received favorable insider treatment in connection with a failed savings and loan company.

- After filing the Whitewater tax returns, he was found dead from a gunshot wound, a possible suicide.
- Despite orders that his office be locked and sealed, files of documents were removed from it by aides of the First Lady.
- A special counsel was chosen to investigate Foster's death and Whitewater. This real estate deal allegedly funneled money to Clinton's campaign in Arkansas.
- The investigation under **Kenneth Starr** was closed in 2000.
- Bill and Hillary Clinton were cleared of any wrongdoing, although Starr won convictions of some Clinton associates related to Whitewater.
- Because of these investigations, Congress declined to extend the Independent Counsel Act when it expired in 1998.
- Bill Clinton was disbarred from practicing law in Arkansas.

Paula Corbin Jones (1994): A state worker who accused Clinton of sexual harassment in May of 1991 when he was Arkansas' governor.
- In January 1998, Clinton was required to testify in the lawsuit and Jones subpoenaed **Monica Lewinsky,** a former White House intern.
- Both Clinton and Lewinsky denied they had had an affair.
- A federal court threw out Jones' suit in April 1998.

1996 election: Dot-com companies, economic expansion, and unemployment rates were the lowest in recent history as the election approached. The recession, inherited from George Bush's administration, had bottomed out in 1994.
- Polls indicated people felt they were better off since Clinton's assumption as president.
- Clinton's charisma also helped him win a decisive victory over Kansas Republican Senator and former Senate Majority Leader, **Robert Dole,** who won only 11 states. Concern about Dole's age (73) surfaced during the campaign.
- Both promised to reduce the deficit but Clinton favored a smaller reduction, so as to spend more on social welfare, the environment, and education.
- Clinton won 379 electoral votes to Dole's 159.
- Republicans lost seats in Congress, but were still a majority in both houses of Congress.
- **Ross Perot** ran again as a third party candidate, receiving 9 percent of the vote.

Key 92   Clinton's second term and
life in the 1990s

OVERVIEW *Clinton's second administration was marked by good economic times and scandal. Unable to run for a third term, Clinton's vice president, Al Gore ran against George W. Bush, resulting in the disputed election of 2000. America continued to evolve in response to a global, service-oriented, high-tech economy.*

The global economy and the computer revolution: Developed as a result of multinational corporations such as Daimler-Chrysler.
- These corporations can avoid tariffs and some regulations that affect profits.
- Aided by the introduction of the Internet, which has changed how people and businesses communicate, keep, and store information, for example, interactive classrooms.
- 13 million new jobs were created because of the computer revolution.
- Our military has been influenced by this new technology.
- Productivity was greatly increased because of the computer revolution and the application of information technology to all stages of the production and distribution of goods and services.
- Pushed the median household income over $40,000 in 1999 and lowered the poverty rate to 11.8 percent.
- The gaps between rich and poor and between rich and middle class failed to narrow.
- Unemployment had fallen to 4.5 percent by August 1998, the lowest level since the 1960s.
- In 2000, a federal judge ordered **Microsoft Corporation** to split up in an antitrust case.

1990 census: Revealed that for the first time in U.S. history, most Americans lived within large metropolitan areas.
- Resulted from the expansion of the economy's service sector dependent upon the growth of management, marketing, research and development, and distribution.
- They consisted of huge semiurban sprawls or suburban cities.
- They grew up around a principal business or economic activity.
- They deepened economic and racial divisions in American society.

Monica Lewinsky: A 21-year-old White House intern who revealed her sexual relationship with the president.
- In a nation-wide broadcast, Clinton denied having sexual relations with her.
- Lewinsky had confided details of her sexual relationship with Clinton to **Linda Tripp,** a former White House employee.
- Tripp secretly tape-recorded 20 hours of conversation and turned them over to special prosecutor Kenneth Starr.
- The tapes contradicted Clinton's and Lewinsky's previous testimony.
- Starr threatened to indict Lewinsky for perjury but offered her immunity if she repudiated her earlier testimony by admitting her sexual relationship with the president and admitting that Clinton and his aides had encouraged her to file a misleading affidavit in the Paula Jones case.
- In August 1997, Clinton testified before a federal grand jury about his relationship with Lewinsky.
- He was accused of lying under oath.
- The **Starr Repor**t accused Clinton of obstructing justice and tampering with witnesses.
- In January 1998, independent prosecutor Kenneth Starr began to investigate the charge that Clinton had sexual relations with Lewinsky and then lied about it to a federal grand jury.
- Clinton finally said that he had "inappropriate intimate contact" with Lewinsky when he testified on videotape to the Starr grand jury.
- Much of his other testimony was filled with legalisms and evasion.
- Lewinsky's detailed testimony was also made public.

Impeachment: In October 1998, the House of Representatives voted to begin a full-scale, open-ended inquiry into possible grounds for Clinton's impeachment. On December 19, 1998, the House voted along party lines to impeach Clinton on charges of perjury and obstruction of justice.
- In January 1999, **Chief Justice William Rehnquist** presided over the impeachment trial.
- Some senators believed Clinton had committed perjury and obstruction of justice but did not consider those actions high crimes and misdemeanors as required in the Constitution for removal of a president.
- The Senate vote was 45 to 55 on the perjury count and 50 to 50 on the obstruction of justice vote.
- Clinton was acquitted of the charges and remained president because the Senate failed to deliver a two-thirds majority vote.

1998 elections: Speaker Gingrich focused on the Clinton-Lewinsky scandal while Starr proclaimed that Clinton's testimony warranted impeachment by the House.

- Democrats gained five seats in the House but Republicans still held a majority of 12 seats. Republicans were unable to increase their 55-45 majority in the Senate.
- Gingrich resigned as Speaker of the House and from his seat in Congress.

Election of 2000: Clinton's vice president, Al Gore, ran against the son of former President George H. W. Bush **[Texas Governor], George W. Bush.** Gore chose Connecticut Senator **Joseph Lieberman,** the first Jew to run on a major party ticket, as his running mate.

- Bush chose **Richard B. Cheney,** who had served in the Nixon and Ford administrations and was Secretary of Defense under Bush's father, as his vice presidential candidate.
- Television news prematurely predicted a Gore victory in Florida and then later announced that the race in Florida was too close to call.
- Florida ballots were in dispute where Bush's brother, Jeb, was governor.
- Uncertainty prevailed for five weeks as Gore asked for a recount of certain counties and Bush challenged the recount in addition to the decision the Florida Supreme Court made in ordering a recount.
- Finally, in ***Bush* v. *Gore,*** the U.S. Supreme Court in a 5–4 vote ruled that the different methods used in Florida counties for recounting the vote violated the Equal Protection Clause of the **Fourteenth Amendment.**
- Since there was no clear-cut state standard for determining the intent of Florida voters, a hand count of disputed votes would be unconstitutional.
- With his 537 vote lead in the popular vote in Florida, Bush won its 25 electoral votes, and the 2000 election.
- Gore conceded the presidency to Bush on December 13, 2000.
- Republicans held a five-vote margin in the House and the Senate was evenly divided.
- This was the first disputed election since the election of 1877, which ended Reconstruction.
- Hillary Clinton became the first First Lady to win public office. She defeated Republican **Rick Lazio** for a U.S. Senate seat from New York.

Clinton pardons: Before leaving office, Clinton issued a series of pardons. Among them was **Marc Rich,** a fugitive commodities trader.

- Denise Rich, Mr. Rich's ex-wife, was investigated to see if she was part of a scheme to buy executive clemency for Rich in return for large campaign contributions to Democratic causes.

Key 93 Foreign policy under President Clinton

OVERVIEW *No new foreign policy had replaced America's post-war containment of communism. What constituted U.S. interests in the world and how those interests should be secured remained unclear, and the United States' role in the interconnected global economy was still not clearly defined. Clinton followed Bush's lead by supporting Russian president Boris Yeltsin, and by sponsoring Arab and Israeli negotiations.*

World Trade Center bombing (February 26, 1993): An explosion ripped through the parking garage of one of the Twin Towers resulting in six deaths and 1,000 people injured.
- A rented van was traced to Islamic fundamentalists.
- **Ramzi Ahmed Yousef,** accused of planning the bombing, was captured in Pakistan in February 1995.
- Returned to New York City for trial, he and three accomplices were convicted and sentenced to life in prison.
- Yousef said his actions were in retaliation for U.S. aid to Israel. He said he was sorry the blast failed to level the tower and kill 25,000 people.

Somalia (1993): U.S. troops were sent here as part of a peacekeeping mission under Bush. In 1993, international forces arrived and the number of U.S. forces declined. American troops left in 1994 after an attempt at political intervention that resulted in 18 U.S. soldiers dead.
- UN troops withdrew in 1995 after failure to set up a stable government.

Haiti (1994): Jean-Bertrand Aristide, a popular priest elected as its head in 1990, was restored to power by the United States. He had been overthrown by General Cedras.
- Former President Carter, Senator **Sam Nunn** of Georgia, and retired General **Colin Powell** went to Haiti and convinced Cedras to step down.
- Meanwhile, 20,000 American forces had arrived in September.
- Aristide returned to Haiti as American troops began to withdraw.

- Although some U.S. forces remained, on March 31, 1995, occupation was turned over to a UN force led by an American general.

North American Free Trade Agreement (NAFTA, approved November 21, 1993): It was a pact between the United States, Mexico, and Canada to eliminate or reduce tariffs and other restrictions on investment and trade over 15 years beginning January 1, 1994.
- Its goal was to improve productivity and living standards by establishing the largest free trade zone in the world.
- Supplemental agreements called for cooperation on labor and environmental issues.

General Agreement on Tariffs and Trade (GATT, 1994): Slashed tariffs on thousands of products throughout the world and phased out import quotas imposed by the United States and other industrialized nations.
- Created the **World Trade Organization (WTO)** (January 1, 1995) to mediate commercial disputes among 117 nations.

Short-term results of NAFTA and GATT:
- The Mexican economy went into a depression and Mexico's workers' wages fell.
- Trade increased but about 142,000 Canadian and U.S. jobs were lost.
- Environmental conditions along the U.S.-Mexican border grew worse.
- Many American employers used the threat of moving plants to Mexico as a weapon in wage negotiations with workers.
- Protests took place in November 1999 against the World Trade Organization when it attempted to meet in Seattle, Washington. Six hundred people were arrested.
  1. Activists were unhappy with the economic and environmental implications of WTO's policies, practices, and agreements.

China Trade Bill (2000): Congress approved and Clinton supported this measure to grant China normal trade relations.
- Clinton issued an executive order requiring an environmental impact review before the signing of any trade agreement (2000).

The Middle East (1993): Israeli and Palestinian foreign ministers signed an agreement at the White House on September 13, 1993. It provided for the restoration of Palestinian self-rule in the Gaza Strip and in Jericho on the West Bank in exchange for land for peace, according to a UN Security Council resolution.
- In 1994, Israel and Jordan sign a declaration of peace on their border with President Clinton present.

Vancouver summit meeting (April 1993): Pledged American assistance to Russian leader **Boris Yeltsin.**

Bosnia: Yugoslavia divided into Serbia, Croatia, and Bosnia, after the collapse of communism. Civil war resulted.
- American troops were part of the NATO peacekeeping forces there.
- An embargo was put on arms shipments to the area.
- Clinton sent food and medical supplies to Bosnians.

Dayton Accords (1995): Brought an end to civil war among Muslims, Serbs, and Croats in Bosnia. Bosnia was divided into a Muslim-Croat federation controlling 51 percent of the territory and a Bosnian-Serb Republic controlling 49 percent of the nation. Basic human rights were restored and free elections were held to appoint a parliament and a joint presidency; 20,000 American troops joined 60,000 NATO troops in Bosnia to enforce the peace treaty.
- In 1998, new fighting broke out in Serbia and NATO launched a bombing attack, carried out largely by Americans.
- In 1999, Clinton sent American troops as part of a NATO force to end the ethnic cleansing of Albanians in Kosovo, which seemed to have been ordered by Yugoslav President **Slobodan Milosevic,** who was voted out of office in October 2000 and was tried in 2002 at the Hague for genocide and crimes against humanity.

Iraq: In 1993, Clinton ordered a Tomahawk cruise missile attack against Baghdad in retaliation for an alleged Iraqi plot to assassinate former President Bush.
- In 1998, Clinton ordered air strikes on Iraqi military installations to punish **Saddam Hussein** for failing to give UN inspectors full access to sites suspected of producing biological and chemical weapons as stipulated in the treaty ending the 1991 Persian Gulf War.
  1. The strikes lasted three days.

"Good Friday Agreement" (April 10, 1998): Ended British rule in Northern Ireland; instituted power sharing between Protestants and the Catholic minority and closer relations between Northern Ireland and the Republic of Ireland. Clinton persuaded the British and Irish to begin this peace process.

Terrorist actions:
  Saudia Arabia (November 1995): A car bomb hit an American military installation in Riyadh.
- Four Islamic militants were convicted and were publicly beheaded on May 31, 1996.

- Another truck bomb destroyed another American military installation in Dharan in retaliation. Nineteen Americans died and 500 were injured.

Africa (1998): Islamic extremists utilized truck bombs at American embassies in Nairobi, Kenya, and Dar Es Salaam, Tanzania.
- About 250 Africans died and 12 Americans were killed.
- Clinton ordered missile attacks on sites in Afghanistan, suspected of being terrorist training camps controlled by **Osama bin Laden,** the Saudi-born millionaire believed to have directed the embassy bombings.
- A factory in Sudan, suspected of being a chemical weapons plant, was also attacked.

***U.S.S. Cole* (2000):** The bombing of this ship in Yemen harbor resulted in the deaths of many Americans.

Other developments:
- In 1994, Clinton promoted the creation of a World Trade Organization, the successor to the **General Agreement on Tariffs and Trade,** a global free-trade system.
- He sent $20 billion in aid to Mexico in 1994 to help its failing economy.
- He supported Russian president Boris Yeltsin although he invaded Chechnya, a crime-ridden ethnic region near Georgia, to prevent its secession.
- He threatened trade sanctions on Japan if they did not lift some restrictions on importation of American goods.
- **Johnny Chung,** a Democratic fund-raiser, revealed that money had been funneled illegally to Clinton's 1996 presidential campaign, which overshadowed talks with the Chinese concerning improved trade relations.

Key 94 The younger Bush presidency

OVERVIEW *George W. Bush is only the second son of a former president to be elected president. Not an outstanding leader at the beginning of his presidency, Bush exercised leadership when the United States faced its greatest challenge on September 11, 2001.*

His agenda: Bush called for tax cuts, prescription drug benefits for elderly and disabled Americans, privatizing **Social Security,** and vouchers for education.

Compromise 11-year tax reduction law: Provided instant $300–$600 rebates to most taxpayers, reduced the four major marginal rates, repealed the estate tax, increased the child-care credit, and provided relief for married couples and incentives for savings.

No Child Left Behind Act of 2001: Required for the first time annual reading and mathematics testing for students in grades three through eight nationwide.
- Required school districts to close the gap between poor and middle-class achievement.
- Mandated failing schools to allot part of their federal assistance to tutoring or providing transportation to other schools.

Campaign Reform Act (March 20, 2002): Its provisions take effect after the 2002 election. They include: banning soft money contributions to the national political parties; increasing individual hard money contribution limits; leaving PAC contribution limits unchanged; and prohibiting corporations, trade associations, and labor organizations from financing "electioneering" ads featuring the names and/or likenesses of candidates close to an election.

Six-Year Farm Bill (May 2002): Raised subsidies of the largest grain and cotton farmers.
- Included $17 billion over 10 years to preserve farmland, save wetlands, and improve water quality and soil conservation on working farms.
- Increased food stamp benefits and restored legal immigrants' rights to them.

Economy: In January 2002, Ford Motor Company announced plans to close five plants, eliminate four models, and lay off 3,500 workers.

- In spite of the government's post-September 11 bailout package, in August 2002, U.S. Airways and United Airlines filed for bankruptcy protection. American Airlines then announced it was laying off 7,000 workers and cutting back its operations.
- America's economic expansion ended by March 2001. The trauma of September 11 caused it to decline further.
- Consumer confidence declined via reduced personal and business travel and entertainment expenses.
- The jobless rate increased in October 2001 and by year's end had reached 5.8 percent, the highest level in six years.

California power shortages: Rolling blackouts took place during January 2001 and the bankruptcy of a major state public utility.
- Help came with state government assistance to the utilities, a cool summer, upgrading of electrical distribution line efficiency, reduced usage due to recession and conservation, and the worldwide energy surplus.

Steel industry: Bush imposed import tariffs as high as 30 percent for three years on steel imports to protect the industry.

Enron: The seventh largest American corporation filed for Chapter 11 bankruptcy protection in 2001.
- It became the largest company in history to fail.
- The company's failure was indirectly related to its long-running exploitation of deregulated markets for wholesale natural gas and electricity.
- Key company officials, while operating largely unregulated marketplaces trading derivative energy contracts, were also running private off-book partnerships and profiting personally, even while they overstated Enron profits.
- On January 23, 2002, **Kenneth Lay** resigned as Enron chairman and chief executive.
- The next day, lawyers investigating Enron's demise reported that **Arthur Andersen,** Enron's auditor, shredded important documents in anticipation of a lawsuit.
- On March 14, 2002, Arthur Andersen was indicted in the Enron inquiry, the first major firm to face a criminal charge of obstruction of justice in the destruction of documents relating to the case.
- Employees lost the most since the majority had retirement funds tied up in near-worthless company stock.

Microsoft: Avoided a court-ordered breakup by settling its antitrust case with the Bush administration Justice Department.

- It had been found guilty of monopolistic practices in a case brought by the Clinton administration and ordered divided into at least two parts.
- After Microsoft allowed computer makers to disable some parts of its Windows operating system and replace them with software from other companies, the replacement judge approved a settlement allowing the company to stay intact.

WorldCom: The second largest long-distance carrier in America lost credibility when a random audit in June 2002 revealed more than $3.8 billion in expenses disguised as profits in 2001 and 2002. Soon after it uncovered $3.3 billion more in bogus accounting. The SEC filed fraud charges against the company and its chief financial officer, **Scott Sullivan,** was fired. The firm submitted the largest bankruptcy filing in United States history in July 2002.

Corporate Fraud Bill (July 2002): The list of companies involved in corporate crime grew. Enron was joined by WorldCom, Adelphia Communications, and ImClone, for example. These business scandals prompted a major corporate fraud bill, designed to overhaul the nation's accounting, securities, and corporate-fraud laws.
- It created a new board to monitor and discipline auditors, established new criminal statutes and longer prison terms to punish executive wrongdoing, and expanded civil court protections for defrauded investors and corporate whistleblowers.

Bankruptcy Law (July 2002): Congress passed a bill to make it more difficult for Americans to escape their debts by filing for bankruptcy.

Privacy rollback (August 2002): Protections for the privacy of medical records adopted by President Clinton were rolled back. New standards no longer required health care providers to get written consent from patients before disclosing or using personal medical information for payment of claims or treatment. Providers will first have to give notice of their privacy policies and procedures.

Supreme Court: Several important decisions include:
- In a 5-to-4 vote, it ruled that the **Boy Scouts of America** had the right to dismiss a troop leader after learning he was homosexual. The right of freedom of association outweighed a New Jersey statute prohibiting discrimination against homosexuals (January 2000).
- The court unanimously declared that federal law prohibited the use of marijuana as a medical treatment for diseases such as AIDS or cancer (2001) *(U.S. v. Oakland Cannabis Buyers' Cooperative).*

- A 6-to-3 majority declared that the death penalty for the retarded should now be termed as cruel and unusual punishment that violates the Eighth Amendment (June 2002).
- In a 5-to-4 decision, the Court upheld the constitutionality of taxpayer-financed vouchers for parochial school tuition. Parents can choose between religious and nonreligious schools (June 2002).
- A 5-to-4 vote expanded the ability of public schools to randomly test students for drugs (June 2002).

Pledge of Allegiance (June 2002): A panel of the U.S. Court of Appeals for the Ninth Circuit, in San Francisco, said the **Pledge of Allegiance** was unconstitutional because the words "under God" (added in 1954) violated the separation of church and state. The decision was immediately stayed and political leaders gathered on the Capitol steps to sing "God Bless America" and to recite the pledge.

World Trade Center and Pentagon attacks (September 11, 2001): On the morning of September 11, the World Trade Center in New York City and the Pentagon in Washington, D.C. were attacked by suicide bombers under the direction of Muslim extremist Osama bin Laden and his **al Qaeda** network.
- A fourth plane, presumably headed for the White House, crashed in western Pennsylvania. It is believed that passengers on board struggled with the terrorists and caused it to crash.
- 189 people died at the Pentagon, 44 in Pennsylvania, and 2,797 at the WTC.
- On May 30, 2002, a silent ceremony marked the end of the cleanup at the WTC site (known as "Ground Zero"). An empty stretcher was carried out representing more than 1,400 of the dead whose remains were not found. A 58-ton steel column was also carried, representing the last of 1.8 million tons of debris.

Response to terrorism: Bush created a cabinet-level position, the **Office of Homeland Security,** to fight terrorism.
- This office coordinates the antiterrorism efforts of 40 federal agencies; Pennsylvania Governor **Tom Ridge** was chosen as its head.
- Colin Powell, Secretary of State, **Donald Rumsfeld,** Secretary of Defense, and **John Ashcroft,** Attorney General, coordinated efforts around the world to fight terrorism as well.
- Other measures: strengthening security at public buildings, upgrading screening at airports, freezing assets of suspected terrorist groups, detaining over 1,000 noncitizens for questioning, allowing Air Force generals to shoot down hijacked civilian

airliners, and granting authority to wartime military tribunals to try suspected alien terrorists.

- In July 2002, the **Federal Aviation Administration** required foreign pilots to submit applications, including a photo ID. The identity of the applicant is verified and the name is checked against various watch lists, making sure the foreign license is valid.
- New Justice Department rules require companies that teach noncitizens to fly large planes to get special permission from the FAA. Noncitizens seeking flight training must undergo criminal background checks and be fingerprinted.
- Foreign pilots will not need a U.S. certificate to fly into the United States.
- In June 2002, the United States received permission to station American customs officials in Rotterdam, Antwerp, and Le Havre to screen cargo headed for the United States for weapons of mass destruction. This system also exists in the Canadian ports of Montreal, Halifax, and Vancouver. The goal is to expand to 20 ports around the world that send the largest volume of cargo to the United States.
- In October 2002, the **North American Aerospace Defense Command** (NORAD) took charge of all military personnel involved in flying patrols over U.S. cities, guarding the waters up to 500 miles off the coast and responding to terrorist attacks. It also coordinates the military's response to forest fires, floods, and hurricanes. This new command also oversees the Joint Task Force Civil Support, which is trained to respond to attacks that involve chemical, nuclear, and biological weapons.

Some perpetrators of terrorism: Zacarias Moussaoui was arrested for conspiring in the September 11 attacks and admitted in a Virginia court that he was part of the al Qaeda network. He claimed he was not directly involved in the plot, and withdrew his guilty plea. French officials believed al Qaeda leaders planned to use him in a follow-up attack.

- **Richard C. Reid** tried to detonate a bomb in his shoe aboard a U.S. airliner.
- **John Walker Lindh,** the 21-year-old Californian who was a soldier with the Taliban in Afghanistan, pleaded guilty to two felony charges and agreed to serve a 20-year sentence.
- **Jose Padilla** was arrested in Chicago after his arrival on a flight from Zurich and held in New York and designated an enemy combatant. He was sent to a military prison in South Carolina. The Justice Department said he was behind a plot to build and set off a dirty radioactive bomb in Washington, D.C., but as of this writing, the FBI has produced no evidence to support this claim.

Congressional response: Granted $15 billion to assist the airlines, including $5 billion in grants.

- $40 billion was appropriated for military activity and assistance to New York City.
- Authorized the use of force to respond to the attacks.
- Provided federal takeover of 28,000 airport security jobs.
- The **U.S.A. Patriot Act** (October 25, 2001) expanded law enforcement powers over money laundering, electronic and telephone eavesdropping, and detention of suspected terrorists, while authorizing increased information sharing and coordination between federal, state, and local law enforcement agencies.
  1. It also provided for the victims of terrorism, public safety officers, and their families in addition to condemning discrimination against Arab and Moslem Americans.
- Thirty-five states named security directors or created task forces to help prevent and deal with terrorism.
- In July 2002, another antiterrorism bill approved $28.9 billion for the Pentagon, rebuilding New York City, improved food inspections, and better FBI computers.

Military response to terrorism: Bush initiated a military assault on the al Qaeda network in Afghanistan and began gathering international support for his actions; 60 nations offered assistance.

- Demands that the **Taliban** turn over its leader **Osama bin Laden** to international forces were met by evasion, then refusal.
- On October 7, 2001, a U.S.-dominated military action began with bomber, cruise missile, and fighter jet attacks throughout Afghanistan.
- Military operations also supported the **Northern Alliance** Afghan resistance fighters.
- In 11 weeks, the Taliban was driven from power and replaced by a UN-brokered coalition, and two women were named as ministers in the government.
- Osama bin Laden was never located, although in June 2002, the Arab language satellite channel broadcast an audiotape of a spokesman for al Qaeda stating that he and his top lieutenant were alive.
- In January 2002, Taliban and al Qaeda prisoners were flown from the Marine base in southern Afghanistan to Guantanamo Bay, Cuba, in the first transport of hundreds of detainees.
- In February 2002, **Mullah Muttawakil,** a high Taliban official, was captured by the United States and an American Taliban soldier, **John Walker Lindh,** was charged with supporting terrorist groups and conspiring to kill U.S. citizens.

- Throughout 2002, U.S.-led assault by ground troops and helicopters targeted remaining al Qaeda and Taliban fighters in eastern Afghanistan.
- An abandoned, partially constructed laboratory was discovered near Kandahar. Notebooks, papers, and videotapes were collected from Afghan training bases and guest houses.
- In June 2002, the traditional tribal meeting convened in Kabul, Afghanistan, with more than1,500 delegates to create a new government. **Hamid Karzai,** leader of the interim government, was elected by a wide majority.
- The United States also turned its efforts to other nations facilitating terrorist activity, especially those believed to be developing chemical, biological, or nuclear weapons.
  1. In January 2002, the Philippines agreed to have U.S. troops train Filipino soldiers to destroy **Abu Sayyaf,** an Islamic terrorist organization.
  2. Similar programs were implemented in Yemen and in Georgia.
  3. In July 2002, Secretary of State Colin Powell announced that the United States would spend $50 million over three years to assist Indonesia in the antiterrorism struggle.

Anthrax threat: During the fall of 2001, several newspaper employees in south Florida contracted the disease by mail.
- Anthrax spores were discovered in the offices of Senate Majority Leader **Tom Daschle,** in post offices, and in several news organizations.
- Most spores were traced to mail from near Trenton, New Jersey.
- Two forms of anthrax had killed 5 people; 14 others recovered.
- No link to the September 11 terrorism acts was established.
- In June 2002, scientists determined that the anthrax powder sent through the mail was fresh, made no more than two years before it was sent.

Another mail scare: In 2002, five pipe bombs exploded near mailboxes in rural areas of Iowa and Illinois, injuring five people. Three more bombs were found. All were accompanied by antigovernment notes. Mail service was suspended and a 21-year-old art student, **Luke J. Helder,** confessed to making the bombs.

Key 95 Foreign policy under the younger Bush

OVERVIEW *Much of his foreign policy was an outgrowth of the events of September 11. Trying to get the rest of the world to combat terrorism was a major goal of his administration.*

Bush blocked U.S. funds to international family planning groups that offered abortion and abortion counseling.

Bush supported creation of a basic missile defense system to be completed by 2004 with additional features to be added later to protect against terrorists and accidental launches.

U.S.S. Greeneville: A U.S. Navy submarine that accidentally hit and sank a Japanese fishing trawler, killing nine people.
- An official apology was issued to Japan.
- Bush called for a review of military procedures.
- Commander **Scott D. Waddle** received a letter of reprimand and was allowed to resign.

China (2001): A U.S. spy plane collided with a Chinese fighter jet off the coast of China.
- The Chinese pilot died.
- The damaged U.S. plane landed and its 24 crew members were held by the Chinese for 11 days.
- Bush sent a letter of apology but did not say America caused the crash.
- China portrayed the letter as taking responsibility for the accident.
- The crew was released, and the remains of the plane were sent back to the United States in July 2001 in a cargo plane.

Bush rejected the Kyoto Treaty, signed by Clinton in 1997, an international agreement to fight global warming.

Middle East: By late 2000, talks between Israeli and Palestinian leaders sponsored by Clinton had fallen apart.
- Violence escalated in 2001 and the Bush administration placed the responsibility for pursuing future negotiations with the Palestinians and Israelis themselves.
- Bush made little progress in getting the two together and after September 11 refused to meet with Palestinian leader, **Yasir Arafat.**

- During 2002, there were almost daily suicide bombings and attacks on settlements, followed by Israeli raids into Palestinian territories, and after June 20, seizure of most West Bank towns.
- In June 2002, Bush declared that Arafat must be replaced before America would support a Palestinian state.

Russia: In 2001, FBI agent **Robert Philip Hanssen** was arrested on charges of having spied for Moscow since 1985. His sentence: life without parole.
- Four Russian intelligence officers working under diplomatic cover in Washington were given 10 days to leave the United States. The Russian ambassador was told that another 46 Russian diplomats must leave by July 1 since they were also believed to be Russian intelligence officers.
- The Russian government ordered American diplomats to leave Moscow.
- Bush and President **Vladimir Putin** signed the biggest arms reduction treaty in history on May 24, 2002.
  1. The accord limits the United States and Russia, within 10 years, to between 1,700 and 2,200 deployed strategic nuclear warheads each.
  2. The United States can store warheads rather than destroy them.
- Bush then withdrew the United States from the 1972 antiballistic missile treaty in June 2002.
- In May 2002, NATO invited Russia to be a nonvoting member. It will not be part of its commitment to "collective defense," and will not have the right to veto new members. A new NATO-Russia Council will focus on counterterrorism, nonproliferation, and containing outbreaks of regional hostilities.

India/Pakistan: During 2002, Hindu-Muslim clashes in western India claimed more than 600 lives. Tensions and military buildups centered on a dispute over **Kashmir.** India was angry over what it saw as American restraint toward Pakistan's failure to control militant groups mounting attacks in Kashmir.
- In January 2002, South Asia bureau chief of the *Wall Street Journal*, **Daniel Pearl,** disappeared while investigating British shoe bomber **Richard Reid's** alleged ties to Muslim fundamentalists. The FBI said a tape delivered to Pakistani officials confirmed the reporter's death. **Ahmed Omar Sheikh,** 28, was sentenced to death for the kidnapping and murder by a Pakistani court. Three other men who took part in the kidnapping were given life terms.
- In March 2002, U.S. agents and intelligence officials raided homes and captured 5 Taliban fighters and 25 Arabs suspected of

being connected to al Qaeda. The Pakistani government sanctioned the operation.

Mexico: A U.S.-Mexico Security Pact, intended to weed out terrorists and smugglers, was approved.

International Criminal Court (May 2002): The United States withdrew its signature from the treaty establishing this court. U.S. officials said the treaty gives too much power to an unaccountable international prosecutor who could initiate cases against U.S. policymakers and soldiers. Bush said he would not cooperate with this court.

Monterrey Consensus (March 2002): Bush and more than 50 heads of state reached this agreement that redefines the relationship between rich and poor nations. It binds poor nations to combat corruption, to open markets, and to respect the rule of law. Rich nations agree to increase aid and reduce barriers to the exports of poor countries. Bush pledged a 50 percent rise in the U.S. foreign aid budget.

G8 Pacts (June 2002): Leaders of the world's largest industrial nations met in Canada.
- They pledged up to $6 billion a year to African nations that enacted major economic and social reforms.
- They also agreed to spend $20 billion over ten years to make Russian nuclear, biological, and chemical weapons more secure.

Trade Measure (August 2002): Congress granted Bush so-called fast-track authority to negotiate trade agreements with other nations that Congress would have 90 days to approve or reject, but not amend. The law also included a 10-year, $12 billion program for helping workers who lose their jobs because of trade.

GLOSSARY

agrarian malaise Discontent among farmers, resulting from changes in their economic position after the Civil War. They sought help from states and the federal government, thus abandoning the doctrine of laissez-faire.

agribusiness Farming that is undertaken as big business, encompassing the production, processing, and distribution of farm products and the manufacture of farm equipment, supplies, and machinery.

American Civil Liberties Union Organization founded after World War I by a group of prominent Americans, including Jane Addams, Clarence Darrow, and John Dewey, to safeguard the constitutional rights of individuals.

amnesty Pardon or forgiveness extended by a government, especially with respect to political offenses.

anarchist One who believes in a government without law or order, or in a government that lacks a central authority.

annexation The process of incorporating new territory into an existing country or state.

assembly line A line of factory workers and machinery on which a product under manufacture passes consecutively from operation to operation until completed.

boycott An agreement to abstain from using or buying a product, or to deal with a firm or person, in order to express protest or to coerce.

bureaucracy An administrative system characterized by diffusion of authority among numerous offices and adherence to rules, forms, and routines.

censure An official expression of blame or disapproval, such as may be made by Congress toward one of its members.

civil service All branches of public service that are not legislative, judicial, or military; a system of government workers who were selected for their positions by means of an examination rather than by political appointment.

closed shop A factory or place of business that employs only union members.

collective bargaining Negotiation between the representatives of organized workers and their employers to determine wages, hours, rules, and working conditions.

conservation Official care, including controlled use and systematic protection, of natural resources such as waterways and forests.

containment United States policy after World War II that attempted to prevent the spread of communism in other areas of the world.

contract labor A worker who comes to the United States under a work agreement.

cooperative An enterprise that is owned jointly by those who use its facilities or services.

deficit The amount by which a sum of money falls short of the required or expected amount. When a government's expenditures exceed income, it is said to have a deficit budget and must borrow funds.

deflation A reduction in available currency and credit that results in a decrease in the general price level.

depression A period of decline in the national economy characterized by unemployment, falling prices, and decreasing business activity.

détente A reduction in tension or hostility, usually between nations, by such means as treaties, trade agreements, or cultural exchanges.

discrimination A display of prejudice or bias; a majority's denial of societal advantages to minority groups.

disenfranchise To deprive an individual of the right to vote or to hold U.S. citizenship.

economic sanction A method of pressure used by one nation to change another nation's policy toward some issue. The pressure is in the form of economic barriers, such as a boycott of particular goods or a complete cutoff of trade.

embargo A government order to limit or halt commerce and shipping in order to influence policies or conduct.

entrepreneur An individual who organizes, operates, and assumes the risk for a business venture.

feminism A movement or doctrine that advocates or demands for women the same rights granted men, such as equal economic or political status.

fraternal organization An association of people linked together by similar backgrounds, predilections, or occupations for a common purpose or interest.

ghetto A section of a city occupied by members of a minority group who live there because of economic or social pressure.

human rights Individual liberties and personal freedoms as embodied in the American Bill of Rights.

immigration The process of entering and settling in a country or region to which one is not native.

impeachment Part of a process of removal of a public official from office. The House of Representatives first presents and adopts formal charges against the official; then the Senate acts as a court to consider those charges. If the Senate convicts the accused, he or she is dismissed from office.

infrastructure The foundation of an organization or system; the basic facilities, equipment, and installations necessary for its functioning.

injunction A court order preventing a person or group from taking a specific course of action; usually applied to an order preventing a union from picketing.

integration A bringing together or unifying, especially blacks and whites in U.S. society; desegregation.

internationalism An ideology that advocates the unity and cooperation of the world's peoples, especially in politics and the economy.

interracial Between, among, or involving different races, especially black and white.

Iron Curtain An imaginary separation between Western free Europe and Communist Eastern Europe, as defined by Winston Churchill in a speech given in Missouri in March 1946.

isolationism A foreign policy that abstains from political or economic alliances or compacts with other nations.

Jim Crow laws Laws that enforced segregation by discriminating against and suppressing black people.

laissez-faire A term used in government and economics during the late nineteenth and early twentieth centuries to mean noninterference or a minimum amount of government regulation of business.

lynching Executing or hanging an individual without due process of law.

mass production The manufacture of goods in large quantities, featuring standardized designs, assembly line techniques, and automatic controlling devices.

military-industrial complex A combination of the Defense Department and U.S. defense industries, utilizing their power to effect an increase in armaments.

monopoly Domination or control of the supply of goods or services in the marketplace by one company or a group.

moratorium An authorization to a debtor permitting temporary suspension of payments

nativism A sociopolitical policy in the United States that favors the interests of native inhabitants over those of immigrants.

New Manifest Destiny The late-nineteenth-century belief that it was the destiny of the United States to expand beyond its continental borders.

PAC Political Action Committees, groups set up by industries or private citizens to lobby the government. Their purpose is to convince representatives, senators, and government officials to support or oppose certain legislation. In short, they push for the approval of legislation, which is in the best interests of the industry or group they represent.

parity Equivalence, maintained by government support of farm-product prices, between farmers' current purchasing power and their purchasing power during a chosen base period.

party coalition An alliance of groups within a permanent political group, organized to promote and support its principles and candidates.

political machine A vote-gathering organization of politicians who loyally support a party boss and get the votes in their neighborhoods to support their party's candidates by fulfilling needs and providing services to constituents.

poll tax A payment required for voting in some states, used as a tactic to keep blacks and poor whites from exercising suffrage.

pooling An agreement between competing businesses to establish controls over production, market, and prices for common profit.

rationing The allocation of food or other scarce items to persons.

rebate A practice, common during the late nineteenth century among railroads competing for the business of major corporations, whereby a part of the amount paid for a product or service was returned to the buyer.

recession A moderate and temporary decline in the economy.

Reconstruction The period (1865–1877) during which the former Confederate states were controlled by the federal government before being readmitted to the Union.

Red Scare Heightened concern, after World War I, in the United States about communism, and fear that it would spread.

relocation The forced resettlement of Japanese-Americans and some Germans and Italians in "relocation" camps throughout the United States during World War II.

remonetization The restoration of silver for use as legal tender.

robber baron A U.S. industrial or financial magnate of the late nineteenth century who became wealthy by unethical means.

segregation The policy and practice of separating the races in, for example, schools, housing, and public places.

sphere of influence An area in which a nation seeks to be dominant by securing preferential treatment of a political, economic, and/or social nature.

subsidy Monetary assistance by a government to a person, group, or commercial enterprise.

suburb A largely residential community around a major city.

suffrage The right or privilege of voting.

tariff A tax or duty imposed by a government on imports or exports.

temperance A reform movement that sought to outlaw the manufacture and sale of alcoholic beverages.

trust A form of business organization in which a group of corporations place their businesses under the directorship of a single board of directors.

Twenty-fifth Amendment Approved in 1967, this amendment provided a procedure to determine how the vice presidential vacancy would be filled and the procedure for determining presidential disability.

United Nations An international organization, founded in 1945, to promote peace, security, and economic development.

victory gardens Plots of land set aside by Americans during World Wars I and II for the cultivation of vegetables so as to limit the purchase of produce in stores.

welfare state A social system whereby the state assumes primary responsibility for the economic and social well-being of its citizens.

yellow dog contract An employer-employee contract in which the employee agrees not to join a union while employed.

INDEX